M000045103

# Who
# Am
# I?

# Who Am I?

## EXPLORING YOUR IDENTITY THROUGH YOUR VOCATIONS

### EDITED BY

# DR. SCOTT ASHMON

*Who Am I? Exploring Your Identity through Your Vocations*

© 2020 New Reformation Publications

All rights reserved. No part of this publication may be reproduced, distributed, or transmitted in any form or by any means, including photocopying, recording, or other electronic or mechanical methods, without the prior written permission of the publisher, except in the case of brief quotations embodied in critical reviews and certain other noncommercial uses permitted by copyright law. For permission requests, write to the publisher at the address below.

Unless otherwise indicated, all Scripture quotations are from The ESV® Bible (The Holy Bible, English Standard Version®), copyright © 2001 by Crossway, a publishing ministry of Good News Publishers. Used by permission. All rights reserved. Scripture quotations marked (NIV) are taken from the Holy Bible, New International Version®, NIV®. Copyright © 1973, 1978, 1984, 2011 by Biblica, Inc.™ Used by permission of Zondervan. All rights reserved worldwide. www .zondervan.com The "NIV" and "New International Version" are trademarks registered in the United States Patent and Trademark Office by Biblica, Inc.™ Scripture quotations marked (KJV) taken from the King James Version.

Published by:
1517 Publishing
PO Box 54032
Irvine, CA 92619-4032

Publisher's Cataloging-In-Publication Data
(Prepared by The Donohue Group, Inc.)

Names: Ashmon, Scott A., editor.
Title: Who am I? : exploring your identity through your vocations / edited by Scott Ashmon.
Description: Irvine, CA : 1517 Publishing, [2020] | Includes bibliographical references.
Identifiers: ISBN 9781945978920 (case laminate) | ISBN 9781945978937 (paperback) | ISBN 9781945978944 (ebook)
Subjects: LCSH: Vocation (in religious orders, congregations, etc.) | Identity (Psychology)—Religious aspects—Christianity. | Christian life.
Classification: LCC BX2380.W46 2020 (print) | LCC BX2380 (ebook) | DDC 253.2—dc23

Printed in the United States of America

Cover art by Brenton Clark Little

# Contents

# Introduction

*Scott Ashmon*

Who am I? What's my purpose in life? How should I live? These questions, however they're phrased, race around in young people's hearts and heads. Parents and peers quiz young people with similar questions: What do you want to be when you grow up? What's your passion in life? What's your major? These questions can be liberating and exhilarating, opening up a world of possibilities and adventure in your life. They can also be confusing and frightening when you're not sure how to address them and worried that your answers won't give you a significant, happy life.

Attempts to answer these big questions about life often follow two paths. One approach is the "constructivist view of identity," where one's life is "asserted" and "ascribed."[1] This approach sees the universe and people's existence in it as fluid and ever-changing, lacking much or any given, essential, and fixed qualities to fill them with meaning and purpose. Because life is formless, any meaning or aim in life must be created by humans. Either people must assert their own identities by creating a reality and identity for themselves or the community must ascribe meaning and identities to people. Often there's a tug of war between individuals and the community over who defines reality and identity. We catch a glimpse of the constructivist view in Justice Sandra Day O'Connor's definition of liberty: "At the heart of liberty is the right to define one's own concept of existence, of meaning, of the universe, and of the mystery of human life. Beliefs about these matters could not define the attributes of personhood [or identity] were they formed under the compulsion of the State."[2]

Another approach to addressing life's big questions can be called the vocational view of identity. This view highlights that there's a profound givenness to the universe and each person's existence. Amid the many God-given choices that people have in life (e.g., what hobbies to pursue, what foods to eat, and which forms of government to set up for a just society), essential ingredients of their identity and purpose are already gifted to them in God's creation, Christ's redemption, their relationships with others, and the callings they receive to care for their neighbors and nature. This received identity reveals to people who and whose they are. It informs their self-understanding, enables them to trust God, and orients them to use liberty to love others as God first loved them in Christ. Douglas Schuurman, a modern American theologian, encourages us toward a vocational view when he writes,

> We need to recover the sense that our lives are in many ways "given" to us by forces beyond our control but ultimately in the loving hands of a provident God. We need also to be aware that the numerous and regular obligations that attend our varied routines and roles are expressions of what God wants us to do in our particular locations, always with a view to serving our neighbor and serving God through our neighbor. . . . The point [of vocation] is not to seek one's self—even one's authentic self. The point is to love God and neighbor, and to take up the cross in the self-sacrificial paths defined by one's callings.[3]

The chapters that follow in this book invite you to explore who you are and to imagine how to live through this vocational lens. The opening chapter introduces the concept of vocation and how it informs your identity and makes you part of a story that's bigger than yourself. The second chapter considers ways to fulfill your vocations virtuously and how doing that leads to the well-being of others and your own happiness. Subsequent chapters address several vocations that young people typically have now or will have later in life: being a student, citizen, neighbor, worker, caretaker of nature, husband, wife, dating partner, parent, child, sibling, saint and priest, and friend. These chapters examine the nature and responsibilities of these roles in light of human and divine wisdom found in the liberal arts tradition and the Bible. The final chapter turns your attention to avocations (or enthusiastic pursuits) in your life, the deep gladness and rest that they give you, and how they can energize and equip you to fulfill your callings.

The end of each chapter includes exercises for reflection and discussion. Many exercises can be done privately. Some are to be done with a partner. All the exercises can be modified for group discussions and activities. However you engage with the questions and ideas in this book, we hope that you gain a greater sense of who you are, are inspired to fulfill your vocations virtuously for others, and experience for yourselves the deep meaning and satisfaction that come with such knowledge and actions.[4]

## Notes

1  Florian Coulmas, *Identity: A Very Short Introduction* (Oxford: Oxford University Press, 2019), 29, 32.
2  Planned Parenthood of Southeastern Pennsylvania v. Casey, Governor of Pennsylvania, 505 U.S. 833 (1992), 851, accessed on March 16, 2020, https://supreme.justia.com/cases/federal/us/505/833/case.pdf.
3  Douglas J. Schuurman, *Vocation: Discerning Our Callings in Life* (Grand Rapids: Eerdmans, 2004), 119, 122–23.
4  Thanks to Dr. CJ Armstrong's INT 100 honors class in fall 2019 for reading the first draft of this book and offering helpful comments on how it could be improved.

# Identity

## A Task or Given?

*Chad Lakies*

### Must You Be Interesting?

Perhaps you've heard of him. He's incredibly famous. His experiences are far beyond anything we might ever be fortunate enough to have. The attention he receives is beyond measure, gaining him invitations and audiences with people who would be inaccessible to you and me. His privileges exceed that of royalty or those with the highest security clearance: in museums, he can touch the art; princesses ask him out on dates; and innovative technology companies clamor for his opinion of their next top-secret product before going public. His mother is so proud of him that she got a tattoo that says "son." "He is the most interesting man in the world."

Perhaps you've seen a commercial by the beer brand Dos Equis that stars the imaginary character. If you haven't, do a quick search on YouTube. Or perhaps you've come across him in an internet meme. Everyone wants to be him. And it just so happens that on the rare occasion he drinks beer, he only drinks Dos Equis.

The brilliant marketers who put this series of commercials together captured something that's true about us all. By the way, it has nothing to do with drinking beer. Some people don't even like beer—and some are underage and shouldn't be drinking it. The commercials' message is less about the beer than we might guess after viewing one of the thirty-second clips.

Rather, the deeper message of the commercials has everything to do with the world we live in, where we interact with others. It has to do with the world in which we try to distinguish ourselves from others as unique. One of the primary ways we do this is through how we appear to others. The marketers at Dos Equis know this about us. To be sure, they are trying to create a unique commercial for their brand of beer. But it's more than just standing out as a unique product or person. The commercials featuring the most interesting man in the world also contain a refrain of what we hear on the invisible airwaves of the culture in which we live. It's a rule, a command, an imperative. To be someone, to be unique, you *must* be interesting.

To be interesting is to garner attention of a certain kind. Interest generates a response in others—they look at us and find us attractive or desirable in some way and therefore acceptable and affirmable. It's almost as if we're not fully human or worthy of life itself until we're interesting. The late writer David Foster Wallace calls it being "watchable." Are we entertaining? Are we impressive? Are we worth looking at? Should people commit their attention to us as opposed to others or other things?

There's a pressure that comes with this imperative to be interesting. It functions like a tyrant. We can't get out from under its domination. And most of the time, we don't want to. We simply go along, taking it for granted that this is the way things are. And it's true—this is the way things are. Standing out and gaining attention has always been a part of being human. We all need to be recognized. This has been true since each of us were babies. Our cries demanded a response. The care that was offered as a result of our cries confirmed our existence. It all happened simply, without much thought. Nevertheless, it was critical for our existence. Such recognition remains so.

The trouble with the search for affirmation, the cultural imperative to be interesting and watchable, is twofold. First, our age of dual existence—our embodied, real-life, flesh-and-blood engagements with others and our digitized projections of ourselves online through avatars, images, texts, sexts, comments, and other virtual forms—exacerbates the various ways we seek approval. While it's normal for humans to need such recognition for a healthy life, we now live in an age when we can, and often do, seek validation around every corner. Second, because we search for affirmation of our lives and identities so prolifically, we're not careful about what kind of confirmation is actually good for us and what kind isn't. Consequently, we're often beleaguered by the constant pressure to appear interesting and watchable—worthy even. Furthermore, we're constantly comparing our own lives to others to see if we're as happy as they are, having the same kinds of amazing experiences as they are, wearing the right clothes, driving the right cars, eating at the right places, hashtagging the right causes, and on and on. And this comparison makes us sad. For some of us, it makes us depressed. For a few of us, it makes us question whether our lives are worthy, whether we should be alive at all. This is where the search for affirmation becomes a problem.

## Who Am I?

It's no question that our identity, our unique individuality as a human being who's different from all others, is a vital part of our existence that we work to establish through our teenage, college, and early adulthood years. Who am I? is a common human question. There are good and bad ways of arriving at answers to that question. One of the more dangerous ways is seeking to establish our identity simply and wholly on the basis of the approval of others. We all do it. Humans have always done it. But ought we to see ourselves only through the eyes of others, adjusting constantly to meet their desires? Or is there another way? Put differently, if we were to more authentically shape the way others see us, what might be the healthiest, most humanly faithful way to do so?

Let's take all this in a more philosophical direction. The German scholar Oswald Bayer helps us think about the challenge of articulating an answer to "Who am I?" by suggesting that we get at this best when we are challenged about something we've said or done. When asked, Why did you do that? we usually want to offer an answer that explains our actions adequately and, furthermore, justifies them—making it appear that we said or did the right thing or, at least, that we did nothing wrong. Bayer discusses this kind of circumstance that we all must endure from time to time: "Those who justify themselves are under compulsion to do so. There is no escape. We cannot reject the question that others put to us: Why have you done this? What were you thinking about? Might you not have done something else? . . . Complaints are made against us. We are forced to justify ourselves and as we do so, we usually want to be right."[1] For Bayer, appearing "right" is a way to appear acceptable. By justifying our words or actions, we're making an effort to convince others that because the things we've said or done weren't wrong or bad, they shouldn't see us as wrong or bad people. Rather, they should perceive us as good and right people. And this should make us acceptable, affirmable. In other words, we have provided an answer to the question, Who am I? by at least saying that we're good people.

Since this sort of social phenomenon repeats itself as we're asked regularly why we did or said this or that, Bayer extends his argument to discuss the social benefit we get from being found acceptable. He goes on to say,

> Only a being that is recognized is a being that is alive. We want con-stant recognition of ourselves because it is vitally necessary. We need its confirmation and renewal. If it is lacking, we try to regain it or even to coerce it. . . . To be recognized and justified; to cause ourselves to be justified or to justify ourselves in attitude, thought, word and action; to need to justify our being; or simply to be allowed to exist without needing to justify our being—all this makes for our happi-ness or unhappiness and is an essential part of our humanity.[2]

Bayer suggests that others perceiving us as acceptable and affirm-able is critical to our happiness. It's so vital that we're even willing to force it, especially when we're not feeling that we have others' acceptance. So we try to fit in—we work to impress, to draw positive attention—all for the sake of regaining that sense that we're wanted, that our identity—our life itself—is worthwhile.

Writing as a Christian, Bayer worries that all our efforts to make ourselves appear acceptable before other humans might in fact be some kind of replacement for a deeper, spiritual problem that we're each trying to solve. That is, if we can make others see us as worthwhile, watchable, desirable, and attractive in some way, do we use the evidence of our wide social acceptability as leverage before

God, suggesting that since humans find us acceptable, how can God think otherwise? Bayer's concern is that our efforts here are merely exhausting us while not actually achieving what we're hoping for and truly desire. So what if there's another way?

## A Bigger Story

I've been teaching and working with young people for about twenty years. One thing that I regularly notice is that they want to be accepted individually for who they are in their own authentic self. And simultaneously, they want to be a part of something bigger than themselves, especially when it comes to their future and the mark they'll make upon the world. I've often found these two desires to be in conflict.

As my students get closer to graduation and anticipate entering the next phase of life, this conflict comes to a dramatic height. Many have been taught throughout their lives the now clichéd phrases that encourage them toward authenticity: Be who you are. March to the beat of your own drummer. Follow your heart. Find your passion. You do you. But as they prepare to launch into the world as an adult with responsibilities, work, bills, and eventually things like a marriage and a family to care for, they have a lot of questions. It seems that all the advice to look inside oneself and to follow one's heart doesn't actually tell a person how to live very well or how to get along with others in the world. While all those clichés sounded lovely and seemed to promise a lot of freedom and opportunity, they didn't offer much real guidance. In particular, they don't say much about what a human life should look like or what it's for. In other words, while we've all been encouraged to embrace our unique individuality, we were taught very poorly about how to be a part of something bigger than ourselves or what that would even look like.

This book is meant to paint a picture of what that "something bigger than ourselves" might be. Furthermore, it will help satisfy our desire for gaining a confident sense of our own individuality by helping us see ourselves and our lives within a bigger picture, a bigger story within which we play a part.

## The Ancient Idea of Vocation

What if we don't have to be *told* how to live? What if what we really need is some help imagining how life might be lived? What if once we have this new picture in mind, we can review our own lives through a new set of lenses, kind of like playing *Pokémon Go* in augmented reality? What if, like the screens on our phones, the new lenses will help us see for the first time something that's already there, not as a virtual thing (like a Pokémon) but as a real, embodied existence where our lives can make sense and feel deeply meaningful?

Within the Christian tradition, there's an ancient teaching called "vocation." We still retain a sense of what vocation means in our everyday language whether we are speaking as Christians or not. But we usually work with a severely narrow sense of what vocation means. In our regular usage of the term, *vocation* is usually synonymous with *job*. So we have "vocational schools" that train students in certain skill sets, enabling them to gain employment in a particular career field, such as working as an electrician.

The ancient teaching has a much broader sense to it. It refers to much more than our jobs while also including them. Five hundred years ago, the biblical scholar Martin Luther helped the people of his day understand that they were chosen by God to make a difference in the world and that their work mattered to God because through it, he was including them in his great story—the redemption of the world. This meant that it was far more than the work humans do in their jobs that mattered; the work done in every area of life mattered. Luther wanted them to see how it was in fact God who was working through them, *in* the work, such that every person is caught up in the ongoing work of God to care for the world.

To make sense of this in our time, it's helpful to define the term *vocation*. Another word we usually use for vocation is *calling*. That's because vocation comes into English directly from the Latin noun for "calling" (*vocatio*). We hear a lot of people wondering about their calling, and occasionally we encounter people trying to find their calling. Some people have a sense about a particular calling, to be a teacher perhaps, or a musician, or a pastor. That a vocation is a calling signals the fact that there's someone doing the *calling*—there's another agent in the mix, someone calling out to you and drawing you toward a particular kind of life. Luther's idea capitalizes on this sense, for he indeed believed that it's God who calls each of us to various, honorable roles in life. And it's important to keep this in mind; otherwise, the idea of a calling, just like the idea of vocation, can lose important sense in our time. As if a calling is just some sort of generic, pie-in-the-sky idea that we talk about with a rather romantic whimsy. As if we're talking about some kind of destiny or fate. But Luther meant nothing like that. He was more concrete. He was specific about the fact that our callings are built into creation, into the ongoing story of God working to care for the world, and that God has chosen to involve humans in that work, using our work itself as he reaches down through us to care for others. Luther discussed this work of reaching down through us as if humans are channels or instruments of God's work. He also described it as humans being the "masks of God."[3] As if God were wearing the human and his or her activity as a mask. In this way, God is hidden but still doing the work of caring for the world. The ancient teaching about vocation, then, is that we are caught up in something bigger than ourselves and invited to see our lives through that lens. When we do that, it changes everything.

Luther's emphasis on understanding vocation in this way was a radical departure from what everyone had previously understood. The people that Luther taught understood vocation narrowly too but in a different way from our contemporary understanding. For them, vocation referred to those who worked for the church in a professional way. Those who were trained and taught to be priests. Those who committed their lives to monasteries and convents, monks and nuns, respectively. Those who were appointed to certain roles, such as bishops and cardinals and even the pope. These roles were vocations, but the idea of vocation was narrowly relegated to roles within the church. There was a sense that those who served in these roles were special, closer to God even, and certainly holier than others on the basis of their particular role. For example, it was believed that those who served in the church wouldn't have to spend as much time in purgatory (a teaching that one had to be "purged" of one's sins after death before finally entering heaven) as everyone else. The unfortunate consequence of this was a kind of social stratification that put those who served in churchly roles in a special class, one that would enjoy power and privilege beyond all others, while everyone else existed in a subordinate class.

Luther was disturbed by this because, as a scholar of the Bible who could read it in its original languages (Hebrew for the Old Testament, Greek for the New Testament), Luther didn't find any teachings in the Bible that legitimated the division of society into these social classes on the basis of how spiritual one's role might be. Rather, he read that God cared equally about the work that everyone did. He saw God give tasks to both of the first humans in creation, calling them to care for the Garden of Eden and the other creatures (see Genesis 1:28–30, 2:15). God also blessed them with the ability to be fruitful and multiply—that is, to bear children. Furthermore, Luther saw that God had called all believers in Christ to be priests, representatives between God and other humans. Luther called this the "priesthood of all believers" (see 1 Peter 2:9).

Notice the two senses of calling here. First, there's the calling that all humans have to care for creation and earth's many creatures, including humans, the pinnacle of God's creations. Our vocations in this sense concern specifically earthly, temporal things—the need for humans to eat, for example, or to promote peace and security for all. Here Luther saw that God called people to unique, honorable tasks that required special skills and abilities that not everyone else had or can have (see Romans 12:3–4). For example, not everyone has an aptitude for cooking, nor does everyone have an aptitude for music. But we all benefit from those who do. Everyone needs to eat, and music is a key part of much of our entertainment and celebration. Likewise, not everyone can teach, nor is everyone able to administrate. But we all benefit from those who can. In the end, God has so arranged the distribution of skills, gifts, talents, and aptitudes that we're able to live together as a society in which all can mutually benefit from the work of one another and even flourish.

A second sense of vocation comes from the idea that all those who trust in Christ as their redeemer from sin and death are made to be priests like Christ. As priests, God uses Christians to call all others to faith in Jesus Christ for the sake of their salvation and even to present themselves as "living sacrifice[s]" for others (see Matthew 28:10–12 and Romans 12:1). Whereas many of our callings are roles in which we are caught up in God's temporally redeeming work through which he cares for creation, the vocation of priests specifically functions to call others to faith and eternal redemption. Christians do this very simply: we tell the story of Jesus and how he has come to bring salvation from death to all through the forgiveness of sins (see John 3:16–17). In other words, just as we become children of God through faith—something that happens because we heard the story of Jesus and believed ourselves (see Romans 10:14–17)—God also uses us to tell the story, to call others to believe. You might say, then, that one of our callings, as Christians, is to call others to hear and believe the gospel of Jesus, who gave his life for us that we might live fully for him.

This picture that Luther started to paint as he taught others about vocation eventually leveled the playing field and erased the old division of society based on whose work was more or less spiritually important. Luther helped everyone see that the honorable work of each person is invaluable to all others and thus equally significant. And since God is at work through us, we could say that all our work is spiritual. We need each other, but for Luther, there was the additional sense that we are also responsible for each other. This too is a radical thought to recover, especially in our time, since we tend to emphasize individuality. Here we return to a point made previously regarding the conflict of the simultaneous desires to live for oneself and to be a part of something bigger than oneself. Both of these can't be true at the same time. Perhaps the fulfillment of human life doesn't come from merely doing what one wants but doing what one has been given to do by playing a part in God's ongoing care for the world. It's like what the Holocaust survivor and scholar of human suffering Viktor Frankl thought: it's not about what I want from life but about what life needs from me.[4] In the ancient teaching of vocation, we can recover a sense of being part of something bigger than ourselves *and* perhaps find that we are able to live a life that's both personally fulfilling and meaningful in a broad sense. In vocation, we can achieve the "eulogy virtues" that aim to make a mark on the world by impacting the lives of others in ways that help them flourish.[5]

## Relationships of Responsibility

Let's explore vocation further. I used to work in food service when I was in high school and for part of college. I know many others, friends and students, who've done the same. Eating is a basic, even primal, act for all humans. Everyone needs to do it. And in our time, we live in a world where there are many involved in getting a meal to our tables, whether we're in our kitchen, at a restaurant, or eating at a food truck. Someone's always doing the cooking, to be sure. But have you stopped to think about all the others involved? There are the farmers who grow food, the baker who bakes it, the factory worker who packages it, the transporter who delivers it, the grocer who sells it, the regulator who makes sure it's safely made, and many more. Each of these people has a role in our getting fed. They play a role in sustaining our lives just by meeting the basic need of providing us a means to our next meal.

At one time in the lives of God's people, God gave them food from heaven (a bread called "manna") and water from a rock (see Exodus 16:1–17:7). If this is the sort of thing that God can do, why doesn't he feed everyone that way all the time? God knows, of course, that humans need to eat. But he doesn't normally do it that way. Instead, he chooses to involve us, much like a father raises a child to help out around the house. Of course the parent could do it all, accommodating the child's every need. But kids want to help, and parents want to involve them. God is doing the same by involving us in his work of feeding others along with ourselves.

Consider another example. In the beginning, God brought humans into existence from the dust of the ground. But he didn't keep on doing it that way. Rather, he immediately involved the humans in the process, blessing them with the ability to multiply, to procreate and have children of their own. To have children is to become a parent. In this way, just like the garden that God gave to the first humans to care for, God called them to care for these new humans, their children. Becoming a parent begins a relationship of responsibility. Vocations are relationships of responsibility to love and to serve others. As we'll see, just like being a parent, every vocation is based on one's relationship to another person who is to be cared for in some particular way. Children need a very unique kind of care.

Consider a final example. Each of you reading this is a citizen of some particular country. While we might all be able to note that citizenship confers privileges of various sorts, it's also a role in which each of us has a responsibility. Perhaps it's paying taxes. Perhaps it's obeying laws. Perhaps it's required military service. Or perhaps it's voting, which is often construed both as a right or privilege and as a duty. To be a citizen is to be in a relationship of responsibility to all other citizens in a particular society, state, or nation. And those responsibilities, when faithfully carried out, function to serve the needs of others in the world around you.

Much of this is all very simple. We take it for granted. Of course good citizens obey laws. Of course parents care for their children. Of course good chefs don't serve rotting food to their customers. Each of these roles is nevertheless a vocation, a calling. Each of these roles is occupied by someone who is part of a much bigger picture, a story that has been in motion since before he or she existed but within which his or her life will be used to impact the world in significant and necessary ways. We might look at all these things and consider them rather mundane, ordinary. But that's just the thing with vocation. Most of the time, our callings have to do with our everyday existence in the world. They're not extraordinary. But they are utterly necessary, significant, meaningful, and often quite fulfilling.

There's an incident reported in the Bible in which Jesus is confronted with a question by a person trying to test him to see if his teachings fit with orthodox beliefs of the Jewish people among whom he lived. He asks Jesus what he must do to inherit eternal life. Jesus rehearses for him the two great commandments that all Jews know: love the Lord your God and love your neighbor as yourself. To this, the man responds, "Who is my neighbor?" To answer this question, Jesus, as he often does, tells a story meant to teach a lesson. Such stories are often called parables. The following is the parable of the Good Samaritan, found in Luke 10:25–37:

> And behold, a lawyer stood up to put him to the test, saying, "Teacher, what shall I do to inherit eternal life?" He said to him, "What is written

in the Law? How do you read it?" And he answered, "You shall love the Lord your God with all your heart and with all your soul and with all your strength and with all your mind, and your neighbor as yourself." And he said to him, "You have answered correctly; do this, and you will live." But he, desiring to justify himself, said to Jesus, "And who is my neighbor?" Jesus replied, "A man was going down from Jerusalem to Jericho, and he fell among robbers, who stripped him and beat him and departed, leaving him half dead. Now by chance a priest was going down that road, and when he saw him he passed by on the other side. So likewise a Levite, when he came to the place and saw him, passed by on the other side. But a Samaritan, as he journeyed, came to where he was, and when he saw him, he had compassion. He went to him and bound up his wounds, pouring on oil and wine. Then he set him on his own animal and brought him to an inn and took care of him. And the next day he took out two denarii and gave them to the innkeeper, saying, 'Take care of him, and whatever more you spend, I will repay you when I come back.' Which of these three, do you think, proved to be a neighbor to the man who fell among the robbers?" He said, "The one who showed him mercy." And Jesus said to him, "You go, and do likewise."

One of the most ambiguous parts of understanding vocation is the fact that our relationships of responsibility extend to our neighbor. Figuring out who our neighbor is tends to be confusing, ambiguous. But from Jesus' parable, we get a sense of how to answer that question fairly easily. Your neighbor is whomever God has put in your path that you have the capacity to help in some manner. Perhaps it's that elderly man in the grocery store parking lot trying to get his groceries into his car's trunk. Perhaps it's the mother pushing a baby in a stroller and trying to wrangle two other small children to a table at a fast-food restaurant while also attempting to carry a tray of food and drinks. These are everyday situations in which it's easy for us to be a good neighbor and offer a helping hand.

In the middle of the twentieth century, a German man named Dietrich Bonhoeffer sailed across the Atlantic to New York City. He had been invited by professors who lived there to be a visiting scholar at their school, but there was a subtler motive at work in their invitation: they wanted to help him escape the horrors of what was happening in Nazi Germany, which was just embarking upon what would become World War II. Bonhoeffer was a Christian, a pastor who studied theology and also taught at the University of Berlin. One of his deepest convictions as a Christian was that all people are created "in the image of God" (see Genesis 1:26–27). This belief caused him to view people in a particular way: when he met any other person, he imagined he was also encountering the divine. That is, by meeting a product of the Creator's hand, he was somehow meeting the Creator. And anything the Creator made, Bonhoeffer was convinced, deserved a particular kind of response: it must be, as it were, handled with care. Bonhoeffer believed that humans should care for others as if they were caring for Jesus, whom Bonhoeffer believed to be God, the divine made man. In fact, Bonhoeffer thought every encounter with another human being demanded this sort of response. It's our responsibility.

Now, there's a way we can play with the word *responsibility*. Rather than thinking about it simply as a "you must" sort of word, we can also think of it as a word pregnant with possibility. For every responsibility, there's also a response-ability. We have the capacity to respond to our neighbors and help them, like the man in the grocery store parking lot or the mom in the restaurant. Or we have the ability to ignore them. No one is coercing us into responding one way or another. We're free to do either. But as Jesus encourages us in the parable, one response is more appropriate than the other. Serving advances the good.

Bonhoeffer felt terribly guilty for leaving Germany at such a dire hour. He could only think of his family, friends, colleagues, and all those strangers who would suffer under the oppressive hand of the Nazis. He didn't believe himself to be so important that such a fate shouldn't befall him as well. So against the advice and concern of his friends who had invited him to America, he quickly left and returned to his own country to see how he might help those who were his neighbors, even if they were strangers. He eventually became a double agent, serving the cause of the Resistance while appearing to work for the Nazis.

On one occasion, he was assigned Operation 7, which was a mission to smuggle seven Jews out of Germany into Switzerland and on to their freedom. This was an interesting test case for Bonhoeffer's convictions, since helping Jewish people meant helping those who disagreed with Bonhoeffer's most deeply held convictions. For example, Bonhoeffer believed that Jesus was the Messiah, the Son of God made man who was sent to save the world from sin, death, and the Devil. And the Jews completely denied the truth of this, believing Bonhoeffer to be fundamentally wrong. Why then would he help someone who believed him to be so deeply mistaken? How could he assist those who disagreed with him so significantly as to cause offense to his most sacred beliefs? He did so because they were his neighbors, however much they didn't share the same perspective on some very important matters. Anchoring his actions and decisions in his Christian identity, he believed it was his responsibility to help them. He could have rejected the assignment. He could have asked for something else to do. He could have sabotaged the operation, resulting in the capture of the Jews and likely their deaths in the concentration camps. But he didn't. He helped them escape to their freedom, and in doing so, he saved their lives.

While helping our neighbor often doesn't result in saving their lives, Bonhoeffer's work in Operation 7 and some of his other work as a double agent did. It also eventually cost him his own life. But he died knowing that he had participated in something bigger than himself. And the goodness of his life has left a mark on our culture because he's known as one of the most significant Christian martyrs in the twentieth century. Having died in his service to others on behalf of Jesus, his life was a witness to what it means to live out a Christian, or priestly, calling by participating in God's work of caring for others.

## Our Multiple, Mundane Vocations

Caring for our neighbor is just one of our vocations. In addition to this, there are several other vocations to consider, such as being a student, citizen, worker, caretaker of creation, family member, saint, and friend. Later chapters in this book will deal with each of these vocations specifically. Here we'll simply note that each of us has multiple callings to serve others in special ways. For example, in your family, you might be a son, daughter, husband, wife, sister, brother, grandfather, grandmother, cousin, aunt, or uncle. Likely you have more than one calling in your extended family. Each role has unique responsibilities of loving service that are central to life in the family. Or, as a redeemed saint and member of God's church, you might be a church worker (e.g., pastor, a director of church music, or a director of Christian education) or a layperson who serves in the church in any number of capacities (e.g., as a treasurer, mission trip leader, Sunday school teacher, or musician in an instrumental ensemble for worship). Each of these roles, like diverse parts of one body, serves the church, the whole body of Christ (see 1 Corinthians 12:12–27).

According to this framework, each of us can see how our own lives have not just one but many vocations. Each of us is living in and fulfilling multiple callings simultaneously, every day. At certain points in life, we'll take on new callings, such as getting a new job or becoming a student again by going back to school for an advanced degree. Here we return to a key point about vocations: the mundane and seemingly ordinary functions of our everyday lives, the things we're always already involved in, are also the very callings and places through which God is reaching down to use us to accomplish his work of caring for others. This means that we're truly involved in significant, meaningful, and fulfilling work, whether that's changing diapers, paying taxes, or planting trees. All of it is God-ordained and catches us up into a story that's much bigger than our own singular lives. This is good and just the way God means for it to be.

## What Happens When I Fail in My Vocation(s)?

Let's admit it. None of us likes to fail, but we all do at some point. It's a cliché, but to fail is to be human. Christians talk about this from the perspective of sin. At bottom, humans are sinful beings, prone to failure because we aren't perfect. Sin should be understood here as something more serious than just eating that dessert you didn't really need. Sin is also not just making a mistake, like spelling a word wrong or calculating the wrong answer in a math problem. Real sin is something other than merely making mistakes. Sin is crossing the line of what God wills for us in our lives, transgressing the boundary of the lives he calls us to live. Christians talk about the boundaries of God's will for our lives when they use the word *law*. God's law tells us how we should live (see, for instance, the Ten Commandments in Exodus 20:1–17). One of the clearest ways that we come to know that we've failed at keeping God's law is when we reflect on our various callings.

Failure to faithfully live out one's calling isn't difficult to identify. The lay theologian Gene Veith offers two helpful lenses to see this: sinning against one's vocation and living outside of one's calling.[6] For example, a spouse ought not to have a romantic or sexual relationship with another person. A parent ought not to abandon a child. A citizen ought not to commit treason. An auto mechanic ought not try to fix your computer. If you're not properly trained, you shouldn't try to fix an electrical problem in your home. Each of these examples involves sinning in or living outside of one's vocation. In some cases, the action is just ineffective. In other cases, the action is sinful because it harms others instead of caring for them.

Let's assume for a moment that you did try to fix some electrical problem in your home. You watched some YouTube video that told you how to fix something yourself. The instructions and demonstration seemed really clear, and the repair didn't seem too difficult. So you thought, "Why hire an expert? I can do this." But you soon find yourself with a burn on your hand from an electrical arc that could have set the house on fire. Of course you're thankful that you're still alive and glad nothing worse happened. But you're also embarrassed and the issue you were trying to fix remains in disrepair. While you might be a homeowner, it's quite clear that you're not an electrician. You failed in your calling as a homeowner by not doing what you ought to have done to care for those in your home and your neighbors: call an expert and allow him or her to safely and properly fix your electrical problem.

We all fail in our vocations. Parents get frustrated and holler at their children when they should respond with patience, reasonableness, and love. Children fail to honor their parents when they ought to follow their counsel and rules. We drive faster than the speed limit allows. We ignore our duty to vote. We don't feel like waking up on Sunday, and so we miss gathering with our fellow Christians in worship. To do any of this is to sin because it neglects the responsibilities of loving service to others that each of us has in our callings and thus violates God's law by not following his will for our lives.

Part of our identity is to acknowledge that we are always already sinners. Because of the rebellion of the first humans' against God in the garden—which shattered humanity's good nature and the unending life they had being created "in the image of God"—and because our own failures, we are born broken and continue that way into death (see Genesis 2:15–17, 3:1–19; Psalm 51:1–5; and Romans 5:12–19). But that's not the last word.

God is patient with us. Because of Jesus, God offers forgiveness for our failures. And he regularly calls us once again to join him in his work of caring for others and the world. This is the remarkable thing about the gospel. Christians are nothing other than feeble, frail, failure-prone people whom God nevertheless saves with his redemptive grace and calls into participatory work alongside him in his Kingdom so that all may come to know him and his love for them. The law that God gives is ultimately beyond our ability to fully keep because we are broken. We are bent toward sin and aimed at death in this life. But God has done something about it. This is the gospel, the good news that proclaims how God has solved the problems of sin and its consequence, death, through the redemptive work of Jesus Christ, who gave his own life in death on a cross to save the life of the whole world. For those who trust this good news, God grants the forgiveness of sins and a new, everlasting life. Sin and death, then, can never fully define us. Our lives take on a different character, a different shape, a different center that holds things together.

Because of Jesus and what he did for us on the cross, our lives come to be cross-shaped and cross-centered. Our failures bring us to the foot of the cross, seeking God's forgiveness. Full forgiveness comes to us there and compels us outward to live a life that's marked by the central experience of grace that we encounter at the cross. Our lives, then, are cross-shaped, molded into a sacrificial servanthood through which God chooses to bring his loving care to others. We receive a new identity at the foot of the cross, where we meet the forgiveness of God offered in the sacrifice of Jesus for us. We become God's children, whom he involves in the work of reconciling the world to himself by extending his love to others through us, both in word and in deed. Because of Jesus, God offers us a new way to understand ourselves. Rather than simply sinners, we are also saints—people redeemed and made holy.

To be clearer about this strange way of talking—describing the Christian's identity as saint and sinner at the same time—let's try this metaphor. There's a battle raging in all of us. We all know that it's better for us to care for others than to be self-centered and concerned only about our own interests. None of us like people who exhibit those tendencies, and we don't like it when we see such tendencies in ourselves. God, through his various callings upon our lives and through the law that he gives to guide our living, is constantly drawing us out of ourselves and toward himself and others. Those who are Christians aren't some holier-than-thou group of people. Rather, they know their failures as a constant reality yet strive to respond to God's call to live for and serve others. The battle, then, is between the sinner that defines the broken nature of every person and the saint that God has made that person to be through redemption in Christ. Saints are people who know the redeeming love of God through faith in Jesus. In this sense, they're not people who are better behaved than others. It's not an identity they've achieved for themselves but one that has been graciously given to them by God on account of Jesus' redeeming work and received through faith (see Ephesians 2:8–10). Thus even Christians battle between living for oneself versus living for others. The good news is that because of Jesus, each of us may turn to God for forgiveness every time we sin against our vocations. Fully forgiven, we go back to our vocations renewed to serve the needs of others around us.

## Identity Isn't a Task; It's Given

One of the primary challenges of our time is the sense that we have to make something of ourselves in order for our lives to be worthy, interesting, acceptable—for us ultimately to be loved. The good news about the ancient teaching of vocation that comes down to us from the Christian church, and Luther's thinking in particular, is that none of the work of crafting an identity is necessary. There's no task for us to undertake in order to become someone who is noticed, accepted, and loved. Rather, you've already been included in something far more important than you could possibly imagine. And it has nothing to do with anything you've done, accomplished, achieved, or anything else. Instead, it has everything to do with the loving heart of the living God who has seen fit to include each of us in his ongoing work of caring for and redeeming the world.

Sometimes we tend to look for God only in the extraordinary. We often use the word *miracle* to describe such a thing. For example, someone is healed from some life-threatening or debilitating condition without medical intervention. Of course we ought to recognize this as a miracle. But God isn't only at work in such extraordinary ways. He's also hidden in the mundane, in the ordinary and everyday labors of people as they do their work. Why, then, should we discount the work of doctors, nurses, and other medical professionals whose care brings about the healing of a person from a life-threatening condition? If God is at work using humans to accomplish good for others, we ought to see the healing of a person by medical professionals as a miracle via ordinary means. From the perspective of the ancient teaching of vocation, this shouldn't surprise us. God is at work in you and in me. And the good that God works in the lives of others through our work, he makes deeply meaningful and fulfilling.

This powerful perspective of vocation prompts us to stop and look again at what we often take for granted. The sometimes dull and dreary ordinariness of life, the mundane world, the simple daily tasks we undertake as students, parents, citizens, and more are all part of a much larger picture. They have an inherent significance, a built-in enchantedness. They're God's work as he reaches down through us to care for others in the world. And through the work of others, he cares for us too.

The rest of this book will help you think more deeply about the big picture that's been painted in this chapter. It will help you see that in many of the typical labors of your daily life, you're caught up in a story that's much bigger than your own life. Your work matters, whatever form it takes. And it always will. God grants this to us because of his love for you and me. Our identity is given to us as his "mask" behind which he's at work caring for the world. What a privilege to be caught up in this grand story!

## Exercises for Reflection and Discussion

1. Discuss with a partner the various ways that you try to get others to see you as affirmable or watchable. Be honest about how you feel when your efforts don't get the desired results—for example, no one pays attention, your post doesn't get many "likes," and so forth. What difference does the argument of this chapter make in considering how much effort we tend to put into shaping our identity and controlling how others perceive us?
2. According to the argument of this chapter, how might you practice perceiving others around you? That is, as opposed to affirming someone simply because he or she appears interesting, how might you acknowledge, honor, and respect that person's identity as someone called by God in ways that are different from yourself and others?
3. Based on this chapter, describe what *vocation* means in a few sentences. Share your definition with a partner. Talk about how the idea of vocation helps you understand what your identity or purpose in life is.
4. Think of the vocations that you have in your family, society, work, and if applicable, the church. From this mental list, pick three specific vocations. For one, draw a picture of a situation where you served another person through that calling. For the next vocation, write a poem about a time when you failed in that role by harming others you had the responsibility to care for. How did you respond to that failure? For the last vocation, describe how God uses others to care for you through that relationship.

## Notes

1 Oswald Bayer, *Living by Faith: Justification and Sanctification* (Grand Rapids: Eerdmans, 2003), 1–2.
2 Bayer, 2–3.
3 Martin Luther, "Exposition of Psalm 147," in *Luther's Works*, American Edition, 55 vols., ed. Jaroslav Pelikan and Helmut T. Lehmann (Philadelphia: Muehlenberg and Fortress / St. Louis: Concordia, 1955–86), 14:114.

4  This thought comes from Frankl's 1946 memoir, *Man's Search for Meaning* (Cutchogue, NY: Buccaneer Books, 1992). On page 85, Frankl writes, "What was really needed was a fundamental change in our attitude toward life. We had to learn ourselves and, furthermore, we had to teach the despairing men, that *it did not really matter what we expected from life, but rather what life expected from us.*"

5  The concept of eulogy virtues comes from David Brooks, *The Road to Character* (New York: Random House, 2015), chapter 1.

6  Gene Edward Veith, *God at Work: Your Christian Vocation in All of Life* (Wheaton, IL: Crossway, 2011), 134–37, 139–41.

# Virtue in Vocation

## The Path to Deep Satisfaction with Life

*Jeff Mallinson*

## Are You Happy?

One morning when I was in elementary school, I found myself quarantined to my room, stuck in bed, and suffering from a miserable bout of the flu. The space shuttle *Challenger* had recently exploded, killing all of its crew. The news kept circling around and around that sad story. I understood it was important, but I was already bummed out, so I switched the channel over to a game show with a big cash prize. Knowing that most of the big-money winners in the lottery, Vegas, or game shows tend to have a bad time of things after their influx of money, I couldn't decide whether to root for or against their attempt to win massive cash prizes. So I changed the channel again. I finally stopped surfing when I came to a public broadcasting station that was running a black-and-white documentary about President John F. Kennedy.

Say what you will about the potential moral failings in the personal life of our thirty-fifth president, and think what you will about his political legacy. As a leader, he represents a bygone era: one in which public figures respected the great questions and ideas of the ages and used the tools they learned from their liberal arts education to seek wise decisions in life. Feverish but interested, I watched as a reporter asked Kennedy a question about his well-being. He had just gone through a rough patch in his career. He had faced down the threat of nuclear annihilation: America's great rival, the Soviet Union, had decided to move nuclear missiles just miles off the coast of Florida to Communist Cuba. Eventually, the crisis was resolved, but it took an emotional and physical toll on Kennedy. The reporter then asked a seemingly impertinent question: "Are you happy that you became president?"

Kennedy's answer involved a reference to ancient Greek thought and the concept of virtue, which I certainly wasn't expecting at the time. And it left an indelible mark on my young mind. Since then, I've tried to find the exact archival footage I watched back then, though to no avail. Nevertheless, because his words had such a profound influence on my thinking about life and purpose, I remembered enough to track down something similar he said to a group of students. He must have spoken about happiness and personal callings in this way in various contexts, but this time, in an address to a group of college students, he conveyed his point well. Kennedy said, "I hope that all of you who are students here will recognize the great opportunity that lies before you in this decade, and in the decades to come, to be of service to our country. *The Greeks once defined happiness as full use of your powers along lines of excellence*, and I can assure you that there is no area of life where you will have an opportunity to use whatever powers you have, and to use them along more excellent lines, bringing ultimately, I think, happiness to you and those whom you serve."[1] The Greek word for this idea is *arete*, which means something like "excellence" but is tied to something (or someone) effectively fulfilling its true purpose with integrity. *Arete* for the Greeks meant excellence in just about anything. Applied to a person's life, however, it is the definition of *virtue*.

In other words, in classical thought, there's an intimate connection between vocation and the moral life. After all, what's the point of being good if it doesn't *do* any good for one's self or others? As Kennedy noted, by understanding our vocation or purpose in life and fulfilling that purpose with excellence, one can be called virtuous, and virtue leads to happiness. The rest of this chapter will explore the nature of virtue as it relates to our vocations in life, especially in light of Christian teaching.

## Happiness Isn't Hedonism

The purpose of a virtuous vocation in life is happiness—happiness both for the person living out his or her vocation and also for the people who benefit from that ethical vocation within society. Sometimes when people hear the term *happiness*, they misunderstand the intended meaning. True happiness isn't pure pleasure and exuberance; that's related to what's called *hedonism*, a philosophy of life that simply seeks to maximize pleasure. True happiness, or at least its highest form, is a deep satisfaction that comes from fulfilling one's callings and the loving connection this creates with other people. It's related to what the apostle Paul meant when he said in Philippians 4:11 that he had learned how to be *content* despite the challenges and trials of life's circumstances.

We should note that while happiness is the highest gift of this earthly life, there's another Christian concept that might be said to transcend it, though it also greatly helps undergird it: *joy*. Joy is the blessed realization of the loving presence and grace of the eternal God. Thus, for instance, the apostle Peter wrote, "Though you have not seen [Jesus Christ], you love him. Though you do not now see him, you believe in him and rejoice with joy that is inexpressible and filled with glory, obtaining the outcome of your faith, the salvation of your souls" (1 Peter 1:8–9). Here we see that it might be possible to have Christian joy without earthly happiness, since joy is based on faith and hope in the eternal, ultimate promises of the gospel of Jesus. Thus it's important, as we consider vocations, that we don't equate a virtuous life with a way to merit eternal life, nor with a purpose in life that's uninterested in eternal things. Sometimes well-meaning Christians think that talk of virtue is unnecessary for grace-intoxicated believers. They're well-meaning because they want to avoid thinking there's anything we humans can do through good works to earn eternal life (see Ephesians 2:8–9). But it's important to note that once we're free from worry about the fear of divine punishment or hope of earning a heavenly reward, we're finally free to do good things that bring earthly happiness to ourselves and others. As Ephesians 2:10 (NIV) goes on to say, "For we are God's handiwork, created in Christ Jesus to do good works, which God prepared in advance for us to do."

Our vocations, then, from a Christian perspective, involve an ethical life in service to the world. This can be good fun once we realize that we're the body of Christ on earth (see 1 Corinthians 12:27) and the temple of the Holy Spirit (see 1 Corinthians 6:19), free to discover multiple vocational ways to heal the world in our everyday lives.

According to this way of thinking, one can be happy without feeling physical pleasure. Consider, for example, a marathoner who is running to raise money for breast cancer research. Suppose he reaches the finish line first despite having recovered from a debilitating injury only a few years prior to the race. Suppose also that the runner is in excruciating knee pain as he reaches the finish line. As friends and family come to embrace and celebrate him, with his hands raised in delight, he's both in physical discomfort and yet simultaneously in a state of deep happiness. His vocation that day was to run. He was successful. And his success brought about something good for people and a cause he cares about. He's thus happy while in pain. This is why so many thinkers over the ages have seen happiness as precious: we can experience it even when life brings us hardships and trials.

Can *anything* in life thwart our happiness? Yes, at least according to the ancient Greek philosopher Aristotle. If happiness comes from fulfilling our callings with excellence but someone or something hinders us from fulfilling that calling, our happiness can be said to diminish. This is why it's important to thoughtfully and prayerfully consider one's vocations and seek ways to fulfill them. How can something thwart our vocations? Often this has to do with liberty in the political and cultural sense. Let's suppose a young woman has a passion for aviation, but she lives in a country where it's culturally impossible to get a pilot's license. She still could find other avenues for happiness, but her happiness would be diminished according to Aristotle. Or suppose there's a young man who is highly intelligent and wants to use his mind to cure cancer as a medical researcher; but then suppose his country experiences a devastating war, through which he finds himself in a refugee camp. Unable to get out and go to medical school, he's stuck in squalor and, unable to fulfill an important calling, his happiness is diminished.

For Christians, the good news is that this isn't the end of the story, and eternal joy is still possible even for a person in the worst of earthly conditions. Nonetheless, since liberty within a society is so important for human flourishing in this life, Christians are invited to promote liberty within their communities, perhaps living out their vocations as voters or public servants, to ensure that everyone within society has access to avenues for them to fulfill their vocations virtuously.

## What Is Ethics and Why Should You Care?

Virtue is a concept from the field of ethics, which is a subject within philosophy dedicated to understanding the nature of goodness and how to achieve it within human life. Ethicists speak of three basic types of moral philosophy: (1) *metaethics*, which asks about the nature of the good in an abstract sense; (2) *normative ethics*, which tries to find methods that will help people make decisions about how to do good, especially when they face moral dilemmas; and (3) *applied ethics*, which focuses on specific controversial issues in concrete contexts, such as whether physician-assisted suicide should be allowed within medical practice.

When it comes to understanding the value of ethics within our vocations, it's usually most helpful to focus on the question of normative ethics. Granted, it might be rewarding to reflect with friends around a campfire about the nature of goodness in the abstract. Nevertheless, society needs moral heroes who, in day-to-day life, are able to deftly and confidently make wise and moral decisions that promote the good and serve to encourage human flourishing for society in general.

There are three basic approaches to normative ethics that philosophers discuss in secular contexts. Before we consider those, let's consider an approach to ethics that makes sense only within a religious framework. Sometimes normative ethics is considered in light of the existence and moral commands of God. Those who believe in a personal God typically care what the ultimate being thinks about human actions, especially if they believe God will judge the living and the dead, calling everyone to account for his or her virtuous and vicious actions on earth. From this perspective, the ethical approach called "divine command theory" makes sense.

Instead of spending time trying to use philosophy to uncover and establish right and wrong, why not just go straight to God's own words and leave it at that? To be sure, not everyone who believes in God trusts a particular holy text to accurately convey what God wants people to do. But for those who do trust in the authority and reliability of a holy book, like the Christian Bible, divine commands are important. Of course, it would be hard or impossible to make a case in a secular public square for ethical teachings in scriptures that not everyone in the community believes. But it at least provides some important guidelines and values for individual believers.

Nevertheless, it's not always possible to simply turn to a Bible verse for quick answers to questions that arise through one's vocations. For one thing, it's often unclear how some of the ancient biblical commands apply to contemporary cultural issues that weren't known to people long ago. People who are employed in the field of cybersecurity, for instance, can look to general biblical principles as they do their work, but they'll also need to use their rational capacities and normative ethical tools in order to determine, say, the extent to which individual privacy should be protected online. Likewise, medical ethics is complicated by the fact that our technology for extending life has grown more and more sophisticated, and in ways unknown to people during biblical times, so there's no way to find a direct Bible verse that addresses how long to keep an elderly, terminally ill, and comatose patient alive through feeding tubes and respirators. There are, of course, biblical values that can be applied to such circumstances, but this requires critical thinking, ethical analysis, and wisdom. In other words, throughout much of life, one of our vocations is to use our minds to make ethical decisions within our primary vocations.

For another thing, many of the ethical quagmires of life involve *dilemmas*. These arise when we're faced with a conflict between two values. For instance, I believe it is good to be respectful of other cultures and their freedom to practice their religions as they see fit, even if I disagree with them. Simultaneously, I believe that women should have equal rights with men within society. Suppose, though, that I'm leading a student overseas study trip to a country that requires women to be accompanied by a man at all times and wear veils over their faces. In such a situation, I would be confronted with a dilemma. If I encourage female students to exercise their freedom and go about town in Western clothing, I support one value while failing to keep with my other value: that cultures should be respected. This is how dilemmas work, and the way to address the dilemma is through normative ethics.

In other words, while divine commands remain important for believers to consider when making moral decisions, whenever perplexing dilemmas arise, we need some additional resource for making tough decisions about how to live in our complex world. For Christians, the Bible definitely provides important ethical standards and concrete teachings, but its most important role is arguably to provide insight into the virtues and moral goals that believers ought to embrace in the first place.

This takes us then to the three classic approaches to normative ethics: *deontology*, *consequentialism*, and *personalism* or *virtue theory*. The first approach, deontology, tries to use reason to identify and follow universal ethical duties. Its most famous representative is Immanuel Kant (1724–1804). Kant formulated what is called the "categorical imperative," which is basically a way of speaking about a universally valid moral duty in two related but different ways. Perhaps the most famous phrasing is this: "Act only according to that maxim by which you can at the same time will that it should become a universal law."[2] Applied to the vocation of an accountant, for instance, we shouldn't fraudulently alter the financial records of our company, since if everyone did that, accounting itself would be an absurd vocation, given that accounting reports would be nothing but various levels of falsehood.

Another version of the categorical imperative is this: "So act as to treat humanity, whether in your own person or in another, always as an end, and never as only a means."[3] This has obvious implications for life within professional vocations. For instance, if someone has the vocation of volleyball coach, she would be acting immorally if she put the future career of an injured player in jeopardy merely to win a high school championship. In most cases, the people we encounter within the context of our vocations are to be the recipients of the benefits of our vocations, not the sacrificial victims of them.

The second approach to normative ethics is consequentialism; it emphasizes the outcomes of an action. It's often associated with John Stuart Mill (1806–73), who developed a form of consequentialism called utilitarianism. His method was to consider, in any given situation, how much happiness would be produced by an action and consider whether the happiness produced would outweigh the potential suffering that same action might produce. Consequentialism is often helpful for making a case within the public square and in politics. Especially in democratic societies, consequentialism produces arguments for behaviors and policies that will maximize happiness and limit sorrow within a culture. In professional vocations, consequentialist considerations abound as leaders within an organization seek to produce a profit without (hopefully) creating too many negative consequences for consumers and the environment.

The third approach is virtue ethics, sometimes called "personalism." For reasons I'll explain shortly, this will be the focus of the rest of this chapter. Virtue theory emphasizes the moral quality of an individual's character. It's often associated with the ancient Greek philosopher Aristotle, but it is arguably one of the oldest forms of ethics and has had many Christian exponents over the centuries.[4] An advantage of virtue theory is that it works toward cultivating moral character within individuals so that whatever perplexing challenges arise in a person's vocation, they'll be able to respond quickly and confidently by drawing from core principles.

While there has been debate over the ages about what characteristics are in fact virtuous, Christians at least can look to Scripture (as mentioned previously) to identify important virtues for believers. For instance, Micah 6:8 (NIV) states clearly that God holds two virtues in high regard: *justice* and *mercy*. To these, Jesus adds the virtue of *fidelity*: "Woe to you, scribes and Pharisees, hypocrites! For you tithe mint and dill and cumin, and have neglected the weightier matters of the law: justice and mercy and faithfulness. These you ought to have done, without neglecting the others" (Matthew 23:23). There are also the so-called theological virtues highlighted by the apostle Paul: *faith, hope,* and *love* (see 1 Corinthians 13:13). Thus Christians living out their vocations are called to do so with such virtues in mind. Remember, though, that none of this has to do with earning a place in the Kingdom of

Heaven. Rather, it's a mark of the way we freely reflect the love of God toward our neighbors, even though believers are never able to achieve moral perfection in this life. The contemporary theologian Mark Mattes observes the following:

> The Christian life is no perpetually reoccurring oscillation between law and Gospel, accusation and liberation. Not oscillation but simultaneity—*simul iustus et peccator* ["simultaneously justified and sinful"]—characterizes Christians, even when they flee from God as wrath to God as mercy. Nevertheless, it is precisely God's Word defining this *simul* that opens another dimension—the horizon of living *outside* oneself, first of all in honoring God, the source of goodness, and second, in serving the neighbor. As new beings, we are not trapped in the oscillation because the Gospel's goal is to effectuate trust in God's promise which allows us to live outside ourselves in God and the neighbor. . . . Discipleship answers not the question "how am I saved?" but instead "what is my life about?"[5]

Thus the reason a virtue approach to ethics resonates well with the doctrine of justification by grace alone, through faith alone on account of Christ alone, is that it focuses on the new identity of believers as new creations in Christ (see 2 Corinthians 5:17) rather than rules by which we would ordinarily judge an individual to be righteous or unrighteous.

To restate the primary forms of normative ethics, then, virtue ethics focuses on the character of the person who acts, consequentialism on the outcomes of particular acts, and deontology considers the quality of the actions themselves. Again, since I believe virtue ethics is the most helpful for making ethical choices within our vocations, the rest of this chapter will explore the connections between virtue and vocation at important junctures of a person's life.

## Virtue and Scholarship

The chapter on the vocation of a student in this book will explore in more depth the nature of this particular calling. Here it will suffice to consider three particular virtues that are important for intellectual cultivation: *honesty, humility,* and *courage.*

The first important intellectual virtue for one's academic vocation is *honesty*. Ethically, our culture seems to be in a stage in which truth doesn't matter as much as what might be described as tribal loyalties. Common ground and common sense seem to be eroding. But the virtue of honesty can address this cultural sickness. Honesty involves a radical respect for the facts, even when they force us to reconsider long-standing beliefs and practices. An example of this is the approach to knowledge and learning that the reformer Martin Luther exemplified. When he first stood against the church and secular authorities at the Diet of Worms (1521), they wanted him to recant his writings about the gospel, but he insisted that it's dangerous to deny what reason and Scripture seemed to present clearly to his mind. So he took a stand for his earnest beliefs, even though it was a frightening move and could have resulted in martyrdom.

Luther held to what he thought he should believe. He said what he thought. Later, when his colleagues at Wittenberg University wanted to explore ideas he thought were silly—like Copernicus and astrology—he allowed them to let the research verify or falsify those theories. In the former case, the new cosmology prevailed. The latter turned out to be a pseudoscience. But in both cases, he was dedicated to truth, not to simply appearing to be smart or right.

If you're thinking Luther was sometimes too honest about what he thought, you have a legitimate point. *Humility*, therefore, is a second intellectual virtue for the scholarly vocation. This isn't the characteristic of timidity, nor is it weakness. It's related to the commitment to truth we've already noted. Humility arises from a recognition that human sin has affected all our faculties, including the mind, will, and emotions. As Paul writes in Romans 1:18, we humans suppress the truth because of our unrighteousness. Even apart from the problem of sin, recognizing the vastness of creation reminds us that we're finite and our limited human perspective can't claim a God's-eye perspective. This is a theme throughout the book of Job, chapters 38–39. God takes Job on a tour of all the wonders of creation that human minds can only begin to know. Consider just one part of that text:

Where were you when I laid the foundation of the earth?
   Tell me, if you have understanding.
Who determined its measurements—surely you know!
   Or who stretched the line upon it?
On what were its bases sunk,
   or who laid its cornerstone,
when the morning stars sang together
   and all the sons of God shouted for joy? (Job 38:4–7)

Humility helps scholars to be open to exhortation, rebuke, and correction. It allows us all to try to understand people with whom we differ. In a practical sense, it also helps us avoid arrogant mistakes within our research and writing. Finally, it has an effect on our ability to share truth with others. If we're humbly and honestly presenting what we believe to be the case, others tend to find that intellectual posture more compelling. Indeed, this was a major reason the early church drew so many to the Christian faith: they were unwilling to be silent about what they thought was true, but they did so with respect for authorities and the larger community, wanting to win arguments not for their own glory but for the sake of their neighbors.

All this culminates in a third intellectual virtue: *courage.* This may not at first seem to have much to do with intellectual life. It's easy to see how courage can help a person climb a mountain, or ride a bull, or act in a local theater production. Intellectual pursuits might seem at first, by contrast, to be quiet and safe endeavors. Yet this isn't the case. In my two decades of working in higher education, I've noticed that academics are particularly afraid of looking like fools and, perhaps more problematically, they're afraid of being scorned for their ideas by other academics. This is a problem when a scholar humbly arrives at a new understanding or theory of the truth but the established authorities reject that scholar's research because it challenges their long-standing ideas.

Consider, for example, the insights of Johann Mendel (1822–84). Working in the field of botany, he developed an important theory of inheritance and was a precursor to the modern science of genetics. His ideas were at first rejected or ignored because they conflicted with the reigning theories of inheritance that were held by the Darwinists of his time. He was able to move general scientific knowledge toward the truth by worrying not about what the dominant scholars thought but rather about what his empirical observation presented to him.

In a sense, these three virtues fit together and help us overcome the vicissitudes of intellectual fads. For instance, with a commitment to *honesty*, virtuous scholars were *humble* enough to be wary of post-Enlightenment modernism's overconfidence in reason and its rejection of the transcendent and supernatural. Later when the so-called postmodern turn occurred—generally, in the late twentieth century—some falsely assumed that truth was entirely elusive, perhaps only the expressions of local communities. Nonetheless, virtuous scholars in that context were *courageous* enough to speak about universal truths, even when it was unfashionable to believe that there were such things.[6]

## Legalism Is for a Job; Virtue Is for a Vocation

Ultimately, while scholarship can be a delight and rewarding pursuit for its own sake, the vocation of scholarship typically involves preparation for life in professional vocations outside the academy. In that context, people typically experience a lot of talk about protocols, procedures, and even professional ethics; there's far too little talk of professional virtue. This, I believe, is because too rarely do professional workplaces see what employees do as a God-given *vocation* and instead see it as a mundane job.

In a vocation, we consider the deeper reason we do what we do. We consider how our vocations are an expression of our loves, our values, and our commitment to cultivating a flourishing community. A job is transactional. It's contractual. And in a contract, we have stipulations or rules we must follow if we want to get paid. Moreover, if a company wants to operate without getting regulatory fines or, what's worse, lawsuits from unhappy customers, certain rules must be followed.

Of course, we generally want there to be rules that will protect us from fraudulent or environmentally harmful corporate practices. Nevertheless, that's only the bare minimum we would hope for from fellow citizens. Focus on the rules such that one is worried not so much about doing harm but more about not getting in trouble is a sign of *legalism*. Legalism assumes that if we establish sufficient and thorough rules, we'll tend to get along and get our regular paychecks. Generally, this works well enough, but sinful humans love to find ways to follow the letter of the law and yet defy the spirit behind those laws.

Consider the financial meltdown and recession of 2007–8. Around this time, people lost their homes, investors lost savings, and real estate prices tanked. Most of this involved behaviors at the root of the overall system that were shady but legal. People were acting in bad faith but not exactly breaking any laws.

For instance, banks didn't sufficiently ask if people could afford the mortgages they were taking out, sometimes accepting misleading "stated income" from mortgage applicants and not requiring "verified income" from these folks. There is, of course, some blame for these individuals who were submitting what they probably thought were white lies. In many cases, these subprime loans they sought would be, in the near term, more affordable than the rent they were already paying. So what could be the harm? Moreover, they were being encouraged to exaggerate their income by lenders who wanted to make a commission.

We could blame the lending industry for the whole mess were it not for the fact that real estate agents tended to spread the false optimism that home values would continue to rise indefinitely. They were unfailingly optimistic, probably even deceiving themselves. Now, if home values keep rising, then giving someone who might not have a lot of earning potential a home loan is an act of kindness, since if he should lose his job and have to sell his home, he might make tens of thousands of dollars or more due to the rising equity of the home.

Surely someone should have seen this coming in the overall banking industry. The problem was that there were many people wanting to invest their money and too few good investments to go around. Arguably, the investors *wanted* the borrowers to fib about their income so the whole money-making system could keep moving.

I'm not trying to offer a low-rent version of economic history here. Rather, I'm trying to illustrate the ways in which sin, lack of virtue, and failure to see one's profession as a noble vocation can lead to human misery. There's one last piece to this cluster of financial vice: the real estate appraiser's vocation. In the real estate industry, there are appraisers whose task it is to ensure that a home loan isn't greater than the actual value of the home to which it's attached. This way, if the borrower defaults on a loan, the bank can recover at least most of its money through a foreclosure sale. In other words, the humble real estate appraiser, often just an everyday individual with a home office, was the last line of defense against the collapse of a whole sector of the economy.

Now, I happen to have close friends and family in the appraisal industry, and before 2007, I don't think they would typically have seen what they did as an important service to humanity. It was, for most of them, a blessing of a job. But it was just a job, not a heroic calling. Unfortunately, many appraisers were encouraged to push the values on homes higher than comparable home sales indicated they should be by people in three other vocations (who probably thought they were mere jobs) I've already mentioned. Real estate agents wanted the values pushed so that they could make the sale and get the commission. Lenders wanted the underwriters to rubber-stamp their mortgage packages so they too could earn a commission. Borrowers wanted appraisers to push the value so they could get their loan and also not have to pay an extra mortgage insurance fee, which is traditionally required for mortgages that involved less than a 20 percent down payment by the borrower. This is because if an appraiser could show that the borrower would have the equivalent of 20 percent equity in the home the moment escrow closed, the bank would likely get its investment back if it needed to foreclose.

Had the everyday appraisers of America decided that their calling was a true vocation, they might have helped us avert a recession. They could have at least mitigated the damage to individual families who often lost their homes when predatory—but still legal—loan payments ballooned beyond their ability to pay them and the values of their homes dipped far below what they owed the banks.

In the aftermath of all this, there were new rules put in place to avoid this ugly mess. For instance, appraisers could no longer be chosen individually by lenders but had to be assigned by a third party. This may have settled things down a bit, though without a commitment to virtue in vocation, sinful humans will almost always find ways to work around the rules or use them to their advantage in vicious ways.[7] In short, a virtuous approach to vocation isn't just good for ethical behavior within a particular profession; it serves to improve the health of society as a whole.

## Good Habits and Preparing for Vocation

As bleak as the professional world may seem, it isn't all hopeless. There are increasingly more employers and industries where character matters. Once, when I was serving as an academic dean at a small liberal arts college, I invited some video production executives to meet with our leadership team. We wanted to discuss whether we should add a video production major to the undergraduate offerings. We also wanted to know what skills they were looking for when hiring recent graduates.

What I found both surprised and gladdened me. They unanimously said that learning about the latest technologies, software platforms, and equipment was of only secondary importance. Instead, they were looking for people who could complete a project with integrity, from start to finish. They wanted people who could be courageously creative and insightful. They wanted people who could capture the truth through the medium of videography, editing, and lighting. In other words, they were looking for students trained in the virtues and competencies cultivated by the liberal arts.

After all, they explained, technologies change and become obsolete rather quickly these days. But the leadership skills of young people who have developed good intellectual and life habits through a liberal arts curriculum are transferrable to most areas of the business. They said they could always get students up to speed on the particular technical platforms they used when they started their on-the-job training. They lamented, however, that it's hard to find employees who are passionate about their callings and have the integrity to complete major projects with excellence.

This insight from contemporary employers fits perfectly with the way Aristotle suggested virtue should be taught in his *Nicomachean Ethics*. He believed that the best way to form virtuous character is to practice it regularly until it becomes part of who we are. Thus by taking one's studies seriously and executing the work involved with integrity, we form ethical habits within our daily lives. Once we enter the workplace or other roles within society, we'll hopefully naturally respond to new challenges and opportunities with those same character traits.

## Leadership toward Virtue in Vocation: Cultivating an Ethos

Aristotle suggested that there's another factor, besides habituation in virtue, that's important for cultivating virtue within a vocation: the cultural values that surround and encourage an individual toward excellence in one's callings. This is called an *ethos*, the character, values, and culture of a society or group. This factor can't be over-emphasized. People tend to be more or less virtuous based on the expectations and values of those around them. While there have been several recent challenges to the methodology of his famous Stanford prison experiment, the research of Philip Zimbardo remains interesting here: he found that otherwise decent people can end up doing pretty ugly things when they're in the wrong context.[8]

By way of application, consider how important virtue is when it comes to law enforcement. Young police officers typically enter the force wanting to do good for the world, to "Serve and Protect" as the motto goes. What a perfect way to express the concept of vocation! Nevertheless, there are notable occasions when we hear news of police corruption, bribery, or excessive violence. How can such things infect a group of "good guys"? The answer tends to be leadership that tolerates a vicious culture.

Suppose you were to get a new job as a police officer. Suppose you want to be a good cop, but all the veterans around you put peer pressure on you to bend some of the rules, and they explain that's just how it's done in the profession. All you know might be that particular culture. You might not have a context for evaluating whether this was a particularly unhealthy ethos or not. But most importantly, you might find yourself doing things your younger self would have found immoral, simply so you could fit in and be liked by your older colleagues. The point is, it's not enough to know what is good from an intellectual standpoint, and it's not even enough to practice virtue before we enter our vocations. To fulfill a vocation virtuously, it's important to consider the culture and peers you'll be working with in a particular calling. As Paul observed, "Do not be deceived: 'Bad company ruins good morals'" (1 Corinthians 15:33).

## The Way of Jesus

Before concluding, let's consider a few bold—but sometimes difficult to understand—teachings of Jesus that relate to important decisions each of us has to make in choosing and fulfilling our vocations.

### Hate Your Parents

This is a startling way of saying something that young adults need to hear when they're thinking about their vocations. It's true that most of us who are lucky enough to have a parent or parental figure ought to be respectful, humbly attentive to wisdom from our elders, and faithful to the command to "honor" your parents (Exodus 20:12). Moreover, Christians are called to love everyone and to not hate. Nonetheless, in many cases, for people to truly follow their life callings virtuously, they'll have to release the fear of disappointing parents and other mentors.

Indeed, Jesus teaches that we aren't just permitted to do what we think we should do with our lives; we might be acting *immorally* if we ignore God's calling for our lives simply to please our families. Jesus says this starkly in Luke 14:26: "If anyone comes to me and does not hate his own father and mother and wife and children and brothers and sisters, yes, and even his own life, he cannot be my disciple."

Now, this doesn't mean that we should have the *emotion* of hatred toward our parents. Rather, I think Jesus is using hyperbole to drive home a point that's hard for us to let sink in. Moreover, it's important to understand the cultural context in which he's operating.

To illustrate, consider the story of a former student of mine who was from a family in South Africa that adhered to the traditional religion that scholars call Yoruba. Her father had several wives, many children, and was an important figure in his village. During the course of her studies, she converted to Christianity and was baptized. Her father took this as extreme disobedience to his authority, and it brought him a sense of embarrassment in light of the scorn of other important men in his village. So he gathered the whole village together for a major event, one in which he sacrificed a goat and called upon the ancestral spirits to withdraw their protection from his daughter, and he even called them to curse her for becoming a Christian.

Despite this, this student was respectful and polite. She eventually came to my university in California. Picking up several part-time jobs in addition to her full-time studies, she was able to set aside some money to send back to her family. Her sense of calling to a professional life in church work provided her with a rewarding career path, and ironically a way to help support her family back home. The example she set for her siblings was positive, and she ultimately gained the respect of her father.

This is precisely the sort of thing Jesus had in mind when he told people to hate their parents. The application for all of us is broad. We should "hate" our high school coaches, youth leaders, pastors, or even our favorite college professors in the sense that we can't let the tyranny of their approval or disapproval sway us from the calling we truly believe is before us. Again, each of these individuals should be consulted when we're seeking wisdom. But there are times when we know what we ought to do; we're just too afraid to upset others in our lives. Paul went so far as to say that we should disregard even an apostle or an "angel from heaven" if they get in the way of the gospel of Jesus (Galatians 1:8).

The practical application of this for college students is particularly important. For instance, when choosing a major—barring the question of whether a parent is funding the education of his or her son or daughter contingent upon a particular course of study—if a student's parents want him to be an accountant but he's passionate about computer science, it's usually best for the student to follow the path that suits his sense of purpose rather than the expectations of parents. To do otherwise, as Aristotle suggested, would be to thwart the path to true happiness.

## Sell Everything

Vocation is a much richer concept than simply the question of one's career track. Indeed, Jesus provides a startling, but transformative, teaching that has great bearing on the question of an individual's vocational discernment. Jesus once spoke the following words to a rich young ruler: "One thing you still lack. Sell all that you have and distribute to the poor, and you will have treasure in heaven; and come, follow me" (Luke 18:22). There's a lot going on here, and in terms of the theology of salvation, this is an example of Jesus pressing the law in an extreme way in order to show a self-righteous religious person that he can't in fact earn a place in the Kingdom of Heaven, since it's a purely gracious gift. Nonetheless, the teaching applies to all of us in an important, albeit often metaphorical, way.

The vocational application of this text is that we can't really serve God and remain virtuous if we measure our lives by false values. Monetary success and worldly wealth are definitely false values. We ought to go further and expand the idea of "selling everything" to include anything that we use to adorn our egos. Fame, power, the domination of others, and prestige in the workplace are all attractive, but they can lead us toward vice. Indeed, there's probably nothing that so often leads people astray in their vocation than the love of money.

I once met an executive at a major US corporation who had been hired to clean up the image and practices of the organization after a major ethical scandal. He explained that the way he was able to behave ethically in the corporate world was by committing, with his wife, to have a cost of living that could be supported if he had to quit his job for moral reasons and had to work a minimum-wage job. After setting three year's salary aside and taking on a modest mortgage that could be covered by a low paying job, he was able to achieve just that. He said there were many times in his career where he was able to overcome the temptation to compromise morally because he didn't have to worry that he'd be unable to feed his family if he took a principled stand.

Here, then, was a person who didn't technically sell everything. In fact, he was pulling in a few million dollars a year. He gave some of it away to charity, but the main point for our purposes is that he was able to fulfill his vocation with excellence—that is, *virtuously*—because he didn't consider money the main measure of his self-worth. He was a Christian, and so he counted on an eternal inheritance, which "neither moth nor rust destroys and where thieves do not break in and steal" (Matthew 6:20). By mentally "selling everything," we begin to see our vocations not merely as ways of earning an income but as ways to become the masks of God in the world, in service to our neighbors.

This isn't a dreary calling: it's an invitation to delight in becoming the people we want to be, not what the world considers to be a successful person. Virtue in vocation is about enjoying one's status as a beloved child of heaven: knowing this, everything else is gravy.

### Put Down the Dishes

Finally, when it comes to the concept of vocation, we must remember we're called to *be*, not, perpetually and frantically, to *do*. The way of Jesus involves peace and rest in the promises of God's unconditional love. Consider the following encounter between Jesus and two sisters:

> Now as they went on their way, Jesus entered a village. And a woman named Martha welcomed him into her house. And she had a sister called Mary, who sat at the Lord's feet and listened to his teaching. But Martha was distracted with much serving. And she went up to him and said, "Lord, do you not care that my sister has left me to serve alone? Tell her then to help me." But the Lord answered her, "Martha, Martha, you are anxious and troubled about many things, but one thing is necessary. Mary has chosen the good portion, which will not be taken away from her." (Luke 10:38–42)

Just like the Jewish Pharisees of his time, Martha was frantically working to make things ready for the Messiah. Most of the Pharisees typically didn't acknowledge Jesus as the Messiah, but they thought that if they could go above and beyond the requirements of the law of Moses, the land would be pure enough for God to send the Messiah to overthrow Roman occupation. Jesus insisted, contrary to this thinking, that they didn't have to *do* anything for God's rescue to arrive. They just had to stop working so hard and notice that God's Kingdom was already at hand.

Now, it is, of course, wise and healthy to tidy things up around the house and do excellent and diligent work in our jobs. Yet sometimes these tasks become false substitutes for true happiness and the joy of receiving the gift of life that God has for us. One of those gifts is rest. Indeed, it isn't off track to suggest that the point of life is life itself, lived with integrity and in gratitude for God's creation.

Despite this gift of life, we too often and tragically whip ourselves into workaholism, especially in the fast-paced economic culture of the US. Theologian and author David Zahl describes this as "seculosity," an American form of religion in which we seek our approval through excessive and relentless work. He writes, "The ultimate reason we work so hard has to do with a harder truth: work has always served as the great American barometer of worth and identity. Our occupation is the number one socially approved means of justifying our existence, and not just the type of occupation but our performance there. When we talk about success or failure in life, it's assumed that we're talking about work, which means that a job is never just a job but an identity. It is where we locate our enoughness, and as such, the spring from which our strictest pieties flow."[9] Zahl's point is that without resting in the grace of God, we find ourselves falsely thinking our career is the primary indication of our value. Instead, we must recognize that the virtuous life engages and then periodically rests from a variety of legitimate and rewarding vocations, all of which pale in comparison to our calling to rest in our identity as beloved children of the Most High God.

## Deep Satisfaction with Life

At the start of this chapter, we considered the ways in which fulfilling our calling with excellence leads both to the well-being of our neighbors and also to a profound form of personal happiness. To conclude this chapter, consider pausing and reflecting on what this means for *your life*, now and in the future. Whatever your age and situation, God is calling you to act in accord with your true identity. Unlike legalistic religious people, who assume that they have to work hard to earn their standing before God, and unlike workaholic secular folks, who assume that they're only as good as their corporate title and pay grade, ethical vocation is itself an invitation to deep satisfaction with life. By fulfilling our callings with excellence—living *virtuously*—we serve a heroic, rewarding role in the grand human story.

### Exercises for Reflection and Discussion

1. Imagine your life twenty years in the future. What accomplishments and meaningful creations might provide you with a deep sense of satisfaction? Capture that image for yourself in a song, short story, or video.
2. Is there anything that stands in the way of you pursuing your true vocation(s) right now? If so, what courageous changes are necessary for you to get on the right course to a happy and fulfilled life?
3. Pick a partner to talk about how the *ethos* of your family, friends, or culture encourages you to act virtuously or immorally. If "Bad company ruins good morals" (1 Corinthians 15:33), what can be done about this?
4. Read Ecclesiastes 3:22. Does our exploration of vocation and virtue help shed light on what the author of this verse is trying to communicate? Is the author being pessimistic, inspiring, or something else altogether?

## Notes

1 "Address at the University of Wyoming. September 25, 1963," in *Public Papers of the Presidents of the United States: John F. Kennedy, Containing the Public Messages, Speeches, and Statements of the President, January 1 to November 22, 1963* (Washington, DC: US Government Printing Office, 1964), 720 (emphasis mine).
2 Immanuel Kant, *Foundations of the Metaphysics of Morals*, trans. Lewis White Beck (Indianapolis: Bobbs-Merrill, 1959), 39.
3 Kant, 47.

4 For a good explanation of how virtue theory applies to life and how it relates to recent social scientific research, see Christian Miller, *The Character Gap: How Good Are We?* (Oxford: Oxford University Press, 2017). I contend that one of the best evangelical classics in virtue thinking—one that differs in significant ways from the Aristotelian and Thomistic versions—can be found in Martin Luther's 1520 treatise, "On the Freedom of a Christian." For a contemporary Christian appropriation of virtue ethics from a Lutheran perspective, see Gilbert Meilaender, *Faith and Faithfulness: Basic Themes in Christian Ethics* (Notre Dame, IN: University of Notre Dame Press, 1991).

5 Mark Mattes, "Discipleship in Lutheran Perspective," *Lutheran Quarterly* 26, no. 2 (2012): 149–50.

6 For the sake of economy, I'm painting with broad brushes here, as they say. I'm well aware that very few Enlightenment thinkers denied human fallibility and likewise very few postmodern philosophers are actually relativists. I'm speaking here more to the way in which *real* scholars avoided the popularized fictions that emerged from more nuanced scholarly proposals. For a bit more detail, see my chapter "How We Know" in *Learning at the Foot of the Cross: A Lutheran Vision for Education*, ed. Joel Heck and Angus Menuge (Austin: Concordia University Press, 2012).

7 I recognize that sin is such that we can't even rely on the concept of virtue here. However, seeking, appointing, rewarding, and hiring people who demonstrate moral integrity with a sense of vocation is surely wiser than relying on sinful people to do the right thing guided merely by red tape and the threat of lawsuits.

8 See Philip Zimbardo, *The Lucifer Effect: Understanding How Good People Turn Evil* (New York: Random House, 2008).

9 David Zahl, *Seculosity: How Career, Parenting, Technology, Food, Politics, and Romance Became Our New Religion and What to Do about It* (Minneapolis: Fortress, 2019), 91–92.

# To Be a Student

## Vocation and Leisure in Service to Neighbor

*Scott Ashmon and Scott Keith*

## The Vocation of Student

A role that many young people have is being a student in a formal educational setting. If you're a young adult, chances are that you're still a student, studying part-time or full-time in a college or university. If you're an older adult, there's also the chance that you're a student again, maybe finishing up your college degree or getting an advanced degree. Surprisingly, even though being a student is extremely common and people spend several years of their lives as students, not as much attention is paid to this calling in life.

So let's ask the question: What does it mean to be a student? Several responses can be given to this seemingly simple question. The place to begin at is the observation that to be a student—like being a citizen, neighbor, worker, caretaker of creation, parent, priest, or friend—is to have a vocation. If you're a college student, this is apparent in the fact that your university has accepted your application for enrollment. In doing so, God, working through the university, has called you, placing upon you the honorable and holy vocation of student.

It might sound strange to say that being a student is holy, but it is. It's much more than, as many people think, merely a path to a profession or financial well-being. Like other vocations, being a student is a God-given role and part of your identity; it's a way for you to respond to God graciously creating and redeeming you by loving and serving your neighbors—and nature—in kind. This love is seen, for instance, when students dive into outstanding scholarship that benefits others' well-being in the best ways possible. It's also seen when students wield their intellect well to compellingly communicate to people the renewed eternal life that Christ freely offers them. Such love is precisely what theologian Stanley Hauerwas hits on in his open letter to college students: "To be a student is to be called to serve the Church and the world. . . . You are called to the life of the mind to be of service."[1]

## Loving Your Neighbor as a Student

How can you love your neighbor as a student? You might immediately jump to doing service projects or going on mission trips. True, these are ways to love others while being a student. But you can do those quite apart from being a student. So the question remains: How can you love others through your calling as a student?

It might be shocking to the system to say this, but the first way to love others as a student is . . . to study. Leland Ryken, a former college president, emphasizes this precise point to students when he says, "Learning, in whatever form, *is* the student's calling."[2] This statement would seem self-evident, since the noun *student* comes from the Latin verb *studeo*, which means "to be devoted to, lay stress on, study." This might seem not only obvious etymologically but also a bit bland. Love, after all, is a transitive, active verb. Studying isn't much of an activity that impacts others, or so it seems.

One might say that studying—learning all that one can and gaining all the wisdom possible—*will* one day result in loving activities. For instance, studying will lead to a degree, which will lead to a job, which will lead to money, which will allow you to care for your family and give to others. This is true, but all vocations have a present vitality to them, not just a future possibility. This means that the calling of a student must also have a present activity of love and service for others.

## Three Ps

This present activity is expressed well in a chapter penned by the historian Korey Mass. Maas talks about the three Ps students serve in studying: parents, peers, and professors.[3] By studying well, students serve their parents' God-given calling (see Deuteronomy 6:4–9 and Proverbs 1:8–9) and personal desire that their children become well-educated for the betterment of themselves, their family, and society. In studying diligently, students lovingly fulfill an obligation to honor their parents for the financial sacrifices they made for their education. Moreover, by studying well, students love their parents now, or in advance, since their studies will put them in a better position to support their parents later when they're old and in need.

Students also love their peers when they study. College isn't just a place. It's a community of colleagues where one student's questions and ideas challenge, shape, and sharpen other students. Every student has a "duty to aid in the enlightenment of one's fellow students."[4] This isn't a new idea about the vocation of a student. It's seen centuries ago in the Spanish scholar Juan Luis Vives's rhetorical question about college: "What greater or closer union can we find than that of the mind of one man who is helped by another man's mind?"[5] This idea is still seen today in concepts like *lateral learning*—a term coined by the American scholar Andrew Delbanco to signal that "students have something important to learn from one another."[6] Such enlightenment doesn't simply happen by bringing different preexisting knowledge and perspectives to bear in collegial dialogue. It occurs by doing what the Reformation-era professor Philip Melanchthon charged his students to do: "I tell you, it is your task to seek the truth."[7] To accomplish this, students must perform two tasks. One, individually pursue knowledge, wisdom, virtue, and beauty. Two, bring the fruits and failures of their labors to their fellow students in and out of class. In this way, studying serves your peers by strengthening their minds and expanding their understanding of life.

The third P is professors. Students also serve and love their professors when they study. College isn't principally about competition; it's about "intellectual cooperation."[8] This holds not just for students working together—sharpening each other's minds instead of dulling them through sloth, cheating, and ignorance—but for students working with their professors. Students love their professors when they jointly share knowledge. Students shouldn't think that they fulfill their vocation simply by attending class, listening to the lecture, reading the assigned text, handing the paper in on time, and the like. Rather, as the nineteenth-century professor John Henry Cardinal Newman said, students should treat college as a "conversation between your lecturer and you."[9] Today, we see this in interactive lectures, lively seminar discussions, invigorating tutorials, and engaging undergraduate research. Bringing your best questions, ideas, and research to class, the lab, and office hours not only fulfills the obligation to serve your fellow students but also fulfills the joint venture with your professor to pursue what's true, good, and beautiful in order to love and serve your neighbors—and nature—now.

## Four More Ps

The three Ps of parents, peers, and professors don't exhaust the people you can love and serve now by studying. To this list, we can add four more Ps: public, past, progeny, and your own person. By learning deeply, students lovingly honor their obligation to the general public, which, like parents, frequently funds their education through state and federal grants so that they become highly knowledgeable, thoughtful, and ethical citizens. Students also love society when—to paraphrase the eighteenth-century American polymath Benjamin Franklin—they use their enlightened minds "to serve Mankind."[10] For instance, students serve their communities when they put their college education to work in using public resources prudently, voting wisely, establishing just laws, carefully exercising individual rights and liberties, and competently contributing to the common good. Students also love society when they use their intellectual tools to observe the communities around them, identify their questions and problems, and research ways to solve them.

Another P you can love as a student is the past. Much education is spent learning the wisdom, folly, ideals, issues, questions, concepts, experiments, discoveries, failures, quandaries, and resolutions of previous people. We investigate the past because it helps us better understand our present and where we might go in the future.

Students can love their intellectual ancestors by listening carefully to them so as to understand them fully, instead of dismissing, neglecting, misinterpreting, and misusing them. To love them, students need to read virtuously. As literature professor Alan Jacobs says, students need to apply the virtue of charity, or loving your neighbor as yourself (see Leviticus 19:18 and Matthew 22:39), when reading, since the "book we are reading is, for the duration of the reading experience, our *neighbor*."[11] Or, as literary critic Wayne Booth paraphrases the golden rule from Matthew 7:12, "read as you would have others read you; listen as you would have others listen to you."[12] Such love moves students to pay careful attention to people in the past, offer fair and honest appraisals of them, and give due credit to their ideas and achievements. By studying this way, students not only love and serve the past, but they also give themselves practice in how to listen charitably to their current and future neighbors.

Progeny are also loved now, or in advance, by students in the act of studying. This can be understood in the simple manner that deeply engaging in your education now will put you in a better position later to gain a good profession that will allow you to provide for your children. But progeny can also be extended metaphorically to communal descendants, all those later positively influenced and affected by what you do now. The history of science, for instance, is full of examples where the basic research that scientists do in the lab is later found to have profoundly beneficial applications in life. At this point, you probably don't know how your studies and research will impact others in the future. We work in the dark, so to speak, when it comes to our future influence. One thing is clear, though. The more we study now, the more knowledge we gain; and the more we learn how to do, the more we fulfill our vocation of student and the more God can use our learning to benefit others later.

Finally, you love your own person when you dive deeply into your studies. While vocations are directed toward loving and serving others, we shouldn't miss how God's command to "Love your neighbor as yourself" presumes that we do—and ought—to love ourselves too. Loving and serving the self only becomes a problem when it turns into selfishness, placing the self above God and others, serving oneself at their expense. But implicit in the command to love is the idea that we do love ourselves and that it's God-pleasing. Indeed,

God cares very much for you, which is why God created you and sent his Son, Jesus Christ, to save you from humanity's fall into sin, shame, sickness, and death and to deliver you to an eternally good life with Him in the new heavens and earth, just like in the beginning (see Genesis 1:1–2:25; 1 Corinthians 15:1–4, 20–26, 50–56; Revelation 21:1–5).

So how do you love yourself by learning? Many students find much personal joy in intellectual adventure and discovery; they love learning itself and how it affects the quality of their lives. Take, for instance, one alumnus of Columbia College. When discussing the value and impact of Columbia's core curriculum at an alumni gathering, several attendees noted how this liberal arts curriculum educated them for citizenship. One alumnus, though, hastened to add that his education "taught [him] how to enjoy life" by opening his mind, eyes, and ears to the beauty around him.[13] Such sentiments aren't novel; they're deeply rooted in the liberal arts tradition. The ancient Greek philosopher Aristotle, for instance, often commented on how personal happiness is found in rationally contemplating reality. We also see the pleasure of study expressed earlier in Scripture, with personal joy coming from meditating on God's teachings (see Psalm 119:47–48 and Jeremiah 15:16).

## Educating the Whole Student

What we've seen so far is that students are first and foremost called to study; this is directly implied in the title "student." Yet students come to college already having multiple vocations. They have families with whom they're very involved. They have jobs that provide them the ability to pay for some of their daily needs. They have friends that mean more to them than many in older generations can imagine. Many of these students participate in sports and athletic endeavors and are highly loyal to those social organizations. In other words, even as students arrive at college, they're loaded down with multiple responsibilities that will influence their academic pursuits.

Oftentimes, these pursuits will come into conflict. Athletic practice might get in the way of studying for an exam. Long hours spent at work might mean that there's less time to spend with one's family, boyfriend, or girlfriend. This conflict often causes a good deal of stress, and even anxiety, within the student. Students today have been pushed to be high achievers, and when individual success isn't achieved in every aspect of life, students often feel high levels of anxiety and even depression.

When college professors and administrators insist that being a student is a college student's primary vocation, many collegians resist, explaining that they have too much to do to consider learning their principal calling. Drawing on the biblical teaching that all people have sacred callings in even the ordinary arenas of life, theology professor Kathryn Kleinhans rightly warns colleges that "insisting that intellectual pursuits are more important than other areas of life can sound a bit like the insistence that the contemplative life of religious men and women is higher than the ordinary life of others." Kleinhans reminds colleges that they're educating whole persons and counsels them to be attentive to students' multiple commitments and social structures as well as the possible tensions that may arise from these varied involvements.[14]

Yet if you're at college full-time, then being a student is one of your primary callings. And if it's the responsibility of colleges to educate the whole student, it's the student's responsibility to participate in all aspects of that holistic education. So how is this done and what does this mean for the student? The answer is a somewhat simple, though not simplistic, two-step approach. First, students need to identify their multiple vocations as well as the requirements those vocations place on them both qualitatively and quantitatively. Again, this is a matter of determining all that you've been called, and agreed, to do and delineating the emotional and time management costs associated with those endeavors. Second, you need to find balance while attempting to avoid what we will call lopsided vocationalism.

## Identifying and Qualifying Your Multiple Vocations

Gene Veith, a lay theologian, identifies that "vocation is played out not just in extraordinary acts—the great things we will do for the Lord, the great success we envision in our careers someday—but in the realm of the ordinary," which includes "washing the dishes, buying groceries, going to work, driving the kids somewhere, hanging out with our friends" and so forth.[15] The life of the student is similarly busy and full of activity both in and out of class. Each of the activities and responsibilities that a student has is a piece of his or her vocational life. With so much going on, it can be difficult or confusing for students to identify what their different vocations are and what kind of commitments each entail.

Vocation is a calling to any number of different occupations, relationships, or commitments. Since the field is so broad, it can be helpful for students to take a moment and identify some of their regular responsibilities. Doing homework, taking out the trash, and calling one's parents are some simple examples of everyday responsibilities of a student. Each of these tasks isn't in itself a vocation but is a part of one. Doing homework is a part of the calling of a student, taking out the trash is part of being a virtuous roommate, and calling one's parents is a part of the vocation of a child.

In order to see just how big a role your various vocations take up in your life, try this short mental exercise. Imagine that you were making a list of all the things you needed to do in a week as opposed to how many hours are available to accomplish those tasks. On the left side, list all the different vocations you have, like student, athlete, musician, friend, and employee. On the right side, note how many hours a week each different vocation takes. How many hours in the week need to be dedicated to accomplishing all your "prescribed tasks"? Keep in mind, if you sleep an average of 8 hours a day, that leaves 112 hours a week to complete all your various vocational responsibilities. Colleges typically expect students to study 2 hours for every 1 hour they're in class. If you're a full-time student taking 15 units of course work in a term, that means being in class 15 hours a week and studying 30 hours outside of class. That's 45 hours a week devoted to learning; that's more than a full-time job. In doing this mental exercise, most students will find that they're seriously out of time to do their studies and all their other tasks. The question, then, becomes not only what are your vocations now but also how do you responsibly balance them all?

## Avoiding Lopsided Vocationalism

Identifying current responsibilities and linking them to individual callings is a good way to get a big picture of the vocations you currently have. But one of the biggest questions for college students is, What will my vocations be after graduation? In other words, Did I pick the right major? Will I get a good job? Will I marry my boyfriend or girlfriend, or will I move back in with my mom and dad? These are serious questions with which students often wrestle. There's no simple answer to these questions, and in fact, most of these parts of life are out of your hands. The future isn't certain, and that's OK because each person has God-given talents and gifts that allow a person to work and find fulfillment throughout his or her changing vocations. Trying to find balance when approaching one's God-given vocations, then, is a better goal than trying to predict the future.

Imagine your life as a bicycle wheel. A bicycle wheel is actually a very complicated piece of machinery. It's made up of several parts: first, there's a hub; second, there are spokes connected to that hub; third, there's a rim that's connected to the spokes and in turn is connected to the hub; and lastly, there's a tire (usually a tube inside the tire as well), which is the part that makes contact with the ground. Each portion of a wheel is important in assisting the wheel to accomplish its primary task—providing a mechanism for the bicycle to move forward. But the hub is the one piece that holds the entire apparatus together. If the tire is flat, the wheel still rolls, though it will take more effort to get and keep the bike moving. If the rim is bent, the wheel can still function, though the ride will be a wobbly one. If a spoke is out of true, the wheel will shake as it rolls, but it will still roll. But if the hub is broken, bent, or even missing, the wheel won't function. It's the hub—the center—that holds everything else in place and makes it possible for the other parts to do their job in turn.

Similarly, a college student has multiple vocations, if he is a full-time student, then being a student is, in a way, his hub. It's a central calling that holds the others in place. The world of a student revolves around studying, learning broadly and deeply. If one of a student's other callings—say, a part-time job—is out of place by taking up too much time, then the student's world may become a bit shaky. It might seem that the hub—being a student—is what's broken. But in

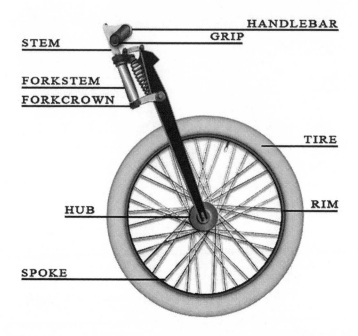

fact, what might be happening is a lopsided vocationalism that puts too much emphasis on an ancillary vocation, which causes the whole student's life to be out of whack. Jobs, family, friends, sports, student leadership, roommates, social time, and the like are all important and need to be dealt with in a student's multiple vocations. But they need to be attended to in balance and with an eye toward what it means to be a college student.

## Activating Your Calling through Leisure

If you're a full-time student, this is the time you've been given to focus on learning. You've been called by God, working through a university, to study. You've also been given an invaluable gift to help you fulfill that calling: leisure.

Leisure is often misunderstood in our modern world. Today we think of leisure as our "time off" to do nothing, just veg out or play video games. But the origin of the word tells another tale. The twentieth-century philosopher Josef Pieper explains that "leisure in Greek is *skole*, and in Latin *scola*, the English 'school.' The word used to designate the place where we educate and teach is derived from a word which means 'leisure'. 'School' does not, properly speaking, mean school, but leisure."[16] What Pieper is driving at is that learning and leisure are intimately connected not just on the level of etymology but in reality. To study, read carefully, ask questions, dialogue, dig deeply, follow an idea, test a hypothesis, discover, create art, hone an argument, craft a paper, master a musical piece, and so on all require leisure in sustained amounts of over extended periods of time.

We can put this into another context to clarify the point. No athlete would think to train just for one day before a competition. Musicians would see it as nonsense to practice once just for a few hours before a performance. Both understand that to fulfill their vocations excellently, they must put in a sustained effort for a prolonged amount of time. To do that, they must have leisure, or free time, from other vocations and use it daily.

The same holds for the vocation of student. To fulfill your calling to study and do it excellently for the benefit of your neighbors and nature, you need to engage in much leisurely activity. You need to find and guard free time every day and week throughout each term to learn.

## Three Types of Learners

Vocational balance, time management, and leisure, though, are just some of the key factors involved in learning. Learning is also about how people study and what motivates them to study that way. What method of study is optimal? The one that helps you learn the most and best fulfill your calling as a student? Consider three types of learners that Ken Bain, currently the president of the Best Teachers Institute, describes in his book *What the Best College Students Do*:

> 1. *Surface learners* are afraid of failure and only do enough to survive the course; scan readings and take notes in class to collect the facts and words that must be memorized to pass the course; prefer lectures that transmit information and answers over class discussions of the

material's meanings and implications; quickly forget
what's learned after "data dumping" for the test; are not
personally invested in their education and uninterested
in how it shapes them; see courses as hurdles to earn a
degree and get a job; and will ask the professor, Will this
be on the test?

2. *Strategic learners* are driven to make high grades in order
   to gain accolades and to get into great graduate schools
   or high profile professions; manage study time effectively;
   master what they think the professor wants them to know
   (terms, facts, theories) and to do (methods, skills, tasks)
   to ace the class; are largely unconcerned with the underlying questions and assumptions of what they're learning
   or its implications and applications beyond class; avoid
   taking on tough courses or knotty problems that might
   jeopardize their grade point average; and will ask the professor, Is there any extra credit I can do to get an A?

3. *Deep learners* are animated by questions, problems, ideas,
   discovery, invention, connecting knowledge from different areas, and figuring out how these impact their lives
   and the world; are less concerned with grades; are not
   afraid of trying new subjects or tackling thorny problems,
   failing in the process, and learning from their mistakes;
   dissect arguments, weigh evidence, and scrutinize conclu-
   sions; question the assumptions and paradigms of others and themselves; seek to challenge and sharpen their
   intellectual abilities and grow personally; and will ask the
   professor, Can we talk about this after class?

You might find a bit of yourself in each type of learner, since everyone can adopt a different study strategy depending on his motivation to learn. Usually, though, a person will employ one method of
studying—surface, strategic, or deep learning.

Which of these learners most fully satisfies the vocation of being
a student? If, as is being argued, the calling of a student is to learn
excellently so that the student can love and serve her parents, peers,
professors, the public, past, progeny, and her own person in the best

ways possible, then being a deep learner is best. If what's needed in life is keenly reading the world around you, accurately spotting the issues facing your neighbors—and nature—carefully analyzing them, and creatively coming up with the best solutions to serve them, then neither surface learning nor strategic learning is sufficient for this calling. Surface learners skim over life looking for easy answers to survive. But life is neither easy nor simply a matter of survival; it's about a flourishing together with truth, goodness, and beauty in our grasp. Strategic learners bring more to alleviate life's plights, since they've mastered many concepts, skills, and procedures. But strategic learners typically have difficulty applying what they've learned to new problems beyond class, since their learning goal was merely to master the material for the class, not to discover how it broadly applies to life. Deep learners best fulfill the calling of a student because they memorize material and master concepts, skills, and procedures as they discern how to address existential questions and protracted problems. They also employ potent intellectual virtues in the process. Chapter two of this book described three of these virtues: honesty, humility, and courage. These and additional intellectual virtues, compiled by philosophy professor Jason Baehr, comprise a collection of "master virtues" used by deep learners. They are the following:

1. *Curiosity*: They examine life deeply by exploring questions and ideas.
2. *Humility*: They don't worry about their intellectual image and admit their ignorance, mistakes, or limitations.
3. *Autonomy*: They can think for themselves.
4. *Attentiveness*: They are deeply engaged in their studies and shun distractions.
5. *Carefulness*: They avoid intellectual traps and think, read, write, and speak with precision.
6. *Thoroughness*: They dig deeper into topics to gain a greater understanding and to offer better explanations.
7. *Open-mindedness*: They consider alternatives and listen fairly to competing ideas.
8. *Courage*: They press on with their questions or ideas despite fears of failure, disagreement, or embarrassment.

9. *Tenacity*: They welcome intellectual challenges and work
   hard to conquer them.[17]

To these, more intellectual virtues could still be added, such as the
wisdom to adapt and to apply what they learned to answer life's
questions and solve its problems. In studying this way, deep learners
might not be more motivated to love and serve their neighbors than
a surface learner or strategic learner, but they wield more and better
intellectual tools to do so.

## What Motivates Learning

If you don't see yourself in the deep learner category, don't panic.
People aren't born as surface, strategic, or deep learners. People
can change their mode of learning. The key is motivation. Surface
and strategic learners are more motivated by external factors such
as grades, degrees, jobs, and honors, hence their learning remains
at that level of what's needed to get these. Deep learners are motivated by three personal factors: curiosity about the world, existential questions, and the pleasure of learning.[18] People who dive deeply
into learning and get the most out of it take personal charge of their
learning, not resting on extrinsic factors to spur them to study. They
look past simply acquiring professional skills or accolades. They seek
to enlighten their minds and souls. They roam around to discover
what interests them. They fashion big questions about life and figure
out how to answer them. They find pleasure in learning, in discover-
ing truth, goodness, and beauty in life. Ironically, while animated by
intrinsic factors, deep learners end up with a widely applicable skill
that all employers prize: the ability to think critically.[19]

Another motivation for excellently fulfilling the vocation of
student comes from the new life and identity that people receive
by God's grace and through faith in Christ (see Ephesians 2:1–10).
Writing to believers in Philippi, the apostle Paul exhorts Christians
to leave aside their previous dishonorable thoughts and actions and,
instead, pursue mental virtues befitting their new life in Christ:
"Whatever is true, whatever is honorable, whatever is just, whatever
is pure, whatever is lovely, whatever is commendable, if there is any

excellence, if there is anything worthy of praise, think about these things" (Philippians 4:8).

The ultimate goal of meditating on what's true, good, and beautiful, though, isn't to get a degree, win academic accolades, or pile up profits for private pleasure. The great goal, as we see from Paul later on, is to use our whole lives to love others as Christ first loved us. As Christ sacrificed his exalted position and life to save us from evil, shame, and death, so we're to respond in faithfulness by being little Christs to others, loving them with our whole being, including our minds. It's in this way that we live out—or "work out" as Paul says—the salvation, new life, and identity in Christ that God has gifted to us:

> Do nothing from selfish ambition or conceit, but in humility count others more significant than yourselves. Let each of you look not only to his own interests, but also to the interests of others. Have this mind among yourselves, which is yours in Christ Jesus, who, though he was in the form of God, did not count equality with God a thing to be grasped, but emptied himself, by taking the form of a servant, being born in the likeness of men. And being found in human form, he humbled himself by becoming obedient to the point of death, even death on a cross . . . Therefore, my beloved . . . work out your own salvation with fear and trembling, for it is God who works in you, both to will and to work for his good pleasure. (Philippians 2:3–8, 12–13)

## Exercises for Reflection and Discussion

1. Get a piece of paper and draw a line down the middle. On the left side, write down all the different vocations you have, such as student, athlete, musician, friend, and employee. In the right column, write down how many hours a week each vocation takes. Do this for all the vocations on your list and then add them up. Remember, there are only 112 waking hours in a week. Do you have more hours in the week dedicated to what you need to accomplish than the hours you're awake? What adjustments in time commitments do you need to make to balance your multiple vocations and live out your student vocation?

2. On the other side of the paper, draw two vertical lines to divide the sheet into three panels. In the left panel, list a pressing problem that you see in your family, society, work, or church. In the middle panel, describe what course of studies or research you could do now to address that issue. Who would you need to work with to make the investigation sound and relevant? In the right panel, identify the people you would present your research findings and proposed solutions to so that this problem can be fixed.

3. Get three chairs. Label one "surface learning," the next one "strategic learning," and the final one "deep learning." Sit in the seat that most reflects how you approach learning right now. Reflect on what motivates you to study that way and the intellectual virtues you use. Be honest. If you didn't seat yourself in the "deep learning" chair, ask yourself, What would inspire me to dig deeper into my studies? What intellectual virtues do I need to master? How can I change how I approach my calling as a student to sit in that seat?

## Notes

1 Stanley Hauerwas, "Go with God: An Open Letter to Young Christians on Their Way to College," *First Things* 207 (November 2010): 50–51.

2 Leland Ryken, "The Student's Calling," in *Liberal Arts for the Christian Life*, ed. Jeffry C. Davis and Philip G. Ryken (Wheaton, IL: Crossway, 2012), 21.

3 Korey D. Maas, "The Vocation of a Student," in *The Idea and Practice of a Christian University: A Lutheran Approach*, ed. Scott A. Ashmon (St. Louis: Concordia, 2015), 103–12.

4 Maas, 107.

5 Quoted in Maas, 107.

6 Andrew Delbanco, *College: What It Was, Is, and Should Be* (Princeton: Princeton University Press, 2012), 54.

7 Philip Melanchthon, "On Correcting the Studies of Youth," in *A Melanchthon Reader*, trans. Ralph Keen (New York: Peter Lang, 1988), 50.

8 Maas, "Vocation of a Student," 107.

9 John Henry Cardinal Newman, *The Idea of a University* (1852; repr., Garden City, NY: Image, 1959), 440.

10 Delbanco, *College*, 65.

11  Alan Jacobs, "How to Read a Book," in *Liberal Arts for the Christian Life*, ed. Jeffry C. Davis and Philip G. Ryken (Wheaton, IL: Crossway, 2012), 129.

12  Quoted in Mark R. Schwehn, *Exiles from Eden: Religion and the Academic Vocation in America* (Oxford: Oxford University Press, 1993), 63.

13  Delbanco, *College*, 32.

14  Kathryn A. Kleinhans, "Places of Responsibility: Educating for Multiple Callings in Multiple Communities," in *At This Time and in This Place: Vocation and Higher Education*, ed. David S. Cunningham (Oxford: Oxford University Press, 2015), 101–2.

15  Gene Edward Veith, *God at Work: Your Christian Vocation in All of Life* (Wheaton, IL: Crossway, 2002), 59.

16  Josef Pieper, *Leisure: The Basis of Culture* (1952; repr., San Francisco: Ignatius, 2009), 20.

17  "Master Virtues," Intellectual Virtues Academy, accessed October 29, 2018, http://www.ivalongbeach.org/academics/master-virtues.

18  Ken Bain, *What the Best College Students Do* (Cambridge, MA: Belknap, 2012), 47–49.

19  "Fulfilling the American Dream: Liberal Education and the Future of Work," Association of American Colleges & Universities, accessed October 10, 2018, https://www.aacu.org/research/2018-future-of-work.

# Living Politically and Globally

*Adam S. Francisco*

## Citizen and Neighbor

What does it mean to be a citizen? Is it about rights? Country of origin? Ethnicity? Religion? How about the concept of neighbor? Who's your neighbor? Is it just the person living next door? What if you don't particularly like them? Words like *citizen* and *neighbor* are so common that it's easy to assume we all know what they mean. But have you ever paused to think what is implied by the term *citizen* and who all counts as your *neighbor*? What we mean and how we understand these common terms are matters of some consequence. They inform how we think and act in the world. So it's worth reflecting on them as we consider the various roles we play in the political and social dimensions of our lives.

## Two Models of Citizenship: Republican and Liberal

The earliest people to reflect on the nature of citizenship were the ancient Greeks. While the rest of the world was divided between rulers and subjects, citizens of Greek city-states enjoyed a measure of liberty and equality unheard of in the ancient world. Because of this, they were convinced that they were distinct from other people. They were a free people; their neighbors—especially the Persians—were subjects, if not slaves, of their rulers.

The Greeks didn't see themselves as a nation or an empire either. Rather, Greece was a land—a peninsula in the northeastern

Mediterranean—filled with hundreds of little states that were the size of a city. The most well-known was Athens. It gave birth to the world's first democracy, and its citizens were intensely proud of it. One of its famous leaders, a man named Pericles (circa 495–29 BC), described it like this:

> Our system of government does not copy the institutions of our neighbours. It is more the case of our being a model to others, than of our imitating anyone else. Our constitution is called a democracy because power is in the hands not of a minority but of the whole people. . . . What counts is not membership of a particular class, but the actual ability which the man possesses. No one, so long as he has it in him to be of service to the state, is kept in political obscurity because of poverty. And, just as our political life is free and open, so is our day-to-day life in our relations with each other. . . . We are free and tolerant in our private lives; but in public affairs we keep to the law. . . . We give our obedience to those whom we put in positions of authority, and we obey the laws themselves, especially those which are for the protection of the oppressed, and those unwritten laws which it is an acknowledged shame to break. . . . Taking everything together then, I declare that our city is an education to Greece, and I declare that in my opinion each single one of our citizens, in all the manifold aspects of life, is able to show himself the rightful lord and owner of his own person, and do this, moreover, with exceptional grace and exceptional versatility.[1]

Public life was political, and the Greeks of Athens took participation in it very seriously. Politics had consequences both in the present and into the future. Thus Athenian citizens—even those not involved in governing or other public work—were "extremely well-informed on general politics." Disinterest was scorned, for it was shameful, and such people, Pericles concluded, had no business living in Athens.[2]

It's no surprise, then, that the most serious reflections on the nature of citizenship in ancient Greece took place in Athens. Aristotle (384–22 BC) wasn't the first, but his *Politics* has proven to be the most influential. In it, he famously asserted that "man is by nature a political animal."[3] That is, like ants, bees, and other animals, humans work together for survival. But more than ants and bees, humans have reason.

When they work together for survival, they also work together toward a common good. That's the goal of the city-state and its citizenry.

However, that doesn't mean everyone living in a Greek city-state was a citizen. There were resident aliens, foreign students, traders, and slaves (like most of the rest of the ancient world). It was amid this diversity that Aristotle and his students asked the question, What's the nature of citizenship? Here's his definition: "A citizen proper is not one by virtue of residence in a given place: for even aliens and slaves may share the common place of residence. Nor [can the title of 'citizen' be given to] those who share in legal processes only to the extent of being entitled to sue and be sued in the courts. . . . The citizen . . . is best defined by the one criterion that he shares in the administration of justice and in the holding of office."[4] By "the administration of justice and in the holding of office," Aristotle means something like participation in the decision-making process of a city-state. That is to say, a citizen is one who has the right and obligation to work with others in public matters—policies of state, legislative affairs, judicial matters, and so on—that will benefit the citizens that make up the city-state. Residents who weren't citizens (or slaves) may have had rights and protections under the law of the state, but they didn't play a role in the politics and governing of it.

This view of citizenship is especially concerned with individuals as political agents with obligations to their polity, whether it be an ancient city-state or a modern nation. It's usually described as a republican (or democratic) understanding of citizenship. It has been described this way: "The key principle of the republican model is civic self-rule, embodied in classical institutions and practices like the rotation of offices. . . . Citizens are, first and foremost, 'those who share in the holding of office. . . .' Active participation in processes of deliberation and decision-making ensures that individuals are citizens, not subjects. In essence, the republican model emphasizes . . . political agency."[5] This notion of citizenship may have emerged in ancient Athens, but it persisted through the ages—in the Roman Republic, medieval Italian city-states, early modern England, and of course, across the Atlantic in its North American colonies. It was here that particular attention was given to the rights and legal status of an individual defined as a citizen in the classical liberal tradition.

The father of this tradition was the English philosopher John Locke (1632–1704). In his *Second Treatise on Government*, Locke argues that because governments are instituted by citizens, rulers of whatever sort govern by consent. Therefore, they're both obligated to respond and to represent the interest of the citizens and bound by a social contract to respect their natural rights.

The founding fathers of America were influenced by Locke and the classical republican tradition. The Declaration of Independence, for example, begins by asserting that "all men are created equal, that they are endowed by their Creator with certain unalienable Rights." Among those rights are "Life, Liberty and the pursuit of Happiness." Governments are thus formed and "instituted among men" to "secure these rights" by the people.[6] And those whose rights are secured by such a government are the citizens of the nation over which that government presides. The Constitution of the United States, especially the Bill of Rights, enumerates specifically what those individual rights are for American citizens.

This is characteristic of what's called the liberal model of citizenship. It "understands citizenship primarily as a legal status."[7] Obviously this doesn't militate against the republican model; in fact, it can work coherently with it. That was what the founding fathers originally aspired to do, though they knew full well that people often choose to assert their rights and freedoms rather than fulfill their political duties and obligations.

This is the inherent weakness of the liberal model. The rights and freedoms it's ordered around are increasingly exercised outside the arena of politics. And thus governance, the making of laws, and so on are accomplished by increasingly distant representatives that often develop into or already are a sort of political class.

Democratic republics like the US require not just wise, honorable, and cultivated people for their preservation as democratic republics. They require wise, honorable, and cultivated people who pursue their duties and obligations as citizens. The rights and freedoms of a citizen, if they're to be protected, must be secured as well as jealously guarded. The American political theorist Michael Walzer writes, "The passive enjoyment of citizenship [in the liberal model] requires, at least intermittently, the activist politics of citizens [in the republican model]."[8]

But the particular political and legal rights, freedoms, and obligations a citizen has are only really meaningful when understood in the context of a particular polity and nation. This is especially true of political obligations. And we should expect a good bit of diversity in this. The duties of citizens in some nations are minor, like serving on a jury and paying taxes. Some require military service. And others require loyalty and subordination to the state.

Political rights of citizens are also quite diverse in different parts of the world. In a democratic republic like America, virtually any citizen can run for public office provided a person meets age and residency requirements. In other republics, there are religious requirements. In Lebanon, the president must be a Christian, the speaker of the parliament a Shia Muslim, and the prime minister a Sunni Muslim. In the Islamic Republic of Iran, a council of religious experts—all Shia Muslims—appoint a supreme leader as the country's topic Shia cleric. He in turn determines who can serve in many of the country's political offices. In monarchies, high political offices are often limited to the royal family, but in a constitutional monarchy like the UK, any qualified citizen can serve in high and low offices—from prime minister to local council member.

The freedoms as well as private and individual rights of citizens are relative to each nation as well. In the US, free speech is guaranteed under the First Amendment. In Canada, it can be and has recently been limited by the government per section 2 of the nation's Charter on Rights and Freedoms. Many western nations consider the freedom to practice religion a basic human right, while other blocs of nations restrict it. In Saudi Arabia, for example, citizens are required to be Muslim. Noncitizen residents are strictly forbidden from the exercise of their religion in public. Over in Myanmar, Muslims can't be citizens and are often brutally persecuted.

The list could go on. The point is that what it means to be a citizen by simple definition is relatively uncomplicated. Reality is different, however, as every nation is sovereign and determines its own policies. What's clear is that, with increasingly rare exception, one's citizenship—and therefore his political and legal freedoms, rights, and obligations—is linked and peculiar to a particular nation. Occasionally it can be extended to two nations, as in the case of dual citizenship. What one can't be, in any politically meaningful sense of the term, is a citizen of the world.

## Global Citizenship?

While the two models of citizenship that have come down to us from centuries past—republican and liberal—are decidedly nationalistic, there has always been a tradition claiming some type of global citizenship that has developed alongside it. Socrates, for example, is said to have declared himself a citizen of the world. While this cosmopolitanism may have begun with him, it was developed into a coherent philosophy more than a century after his death when the political landscape in the Greek-speaking world had changed from being centered on each individual city-state to a world (a cosmos) that was viewed as a super city-state by the conquests of a young, Greek-educated Macedonian named Alexander the Great (356–22 BC). The philosophical tradition behind it was called Stoicism. Animated more by considerations of how one ought to live rather than speculation on what constitutes ultimate reality, it was concerned with politics as much as ethics.

The Stoics of the Hellenistic age taught that being good required serving others and serving humanity as a whole. The most beneficial service was political. However, because the world they inhabited was no longer divided into small city-states, they knew political engagement wouldn't be "possible for everyone . . . [so] some people will best be able to help other human beings as private teachers of virtue rather than as politicians." Nevertheless, those capable of serving in political offices shouldn't do so merely with a view toward benefiting local interests. "The motivating idea is, after all, to help human beings as such," explain philosophers Pauline Kleingeld and Eric Brown, "and sometimes the best way to do that is to serve as a teacher or as a political advisor in some foreign place. In this fashion, the Stoics introduce clear, practical content to their metaphor of the cosmopolis: a cosmopolitan considers moving away in order to serve, whereas a non-cosmopolitan does not."[9] Elsewhere, especially in the increasingly urban world of Rome, Stoics taught that one could approach local matters in view of and with respect to the larger Mediterranean world and beyond. The goal of Stoicism was, nevertheless, the same: to improve the lives of citizens in a particular city or the transcontinental world of the Roman Empire.

After the so-called fall of Rome in the fifth century AD, cosmopolitanism disappeared. It wouldn't have made sense anyway, as the empire defined as the cosmopolis ceased to exist. Politics were local again. Reflections on citizenship were limited. Where they did exist, they were shaped by the ideas of Aristotle (especially beginning in the twelfth century). But toward the end of the Middle Ages, cosmopolitan views began to merge once again. The famous renaissance humanist Erasmus of Rotterdam (1466–1536) discovered it in ancient Greek and Latin texts and began to emphasize the essential unity of humanity across a religiously and politically divided world. In *The Complaint of Peace*, Erasmus appealed to like-minded world citizens and pleaded for the setting aside of differences and intolerances so that the world might realize its destiny of world peace.

Two centuries later, as nation-states were becoming the norm, one of the most specific, yet idealistic, proposals for a cosmopolitanism was put forward by a Prussian anarchist known as Anacharsis Cloots (1755–94). Cloots advocated for the abolition of governments and geopolitical borders and, in their place, the creation of a world-state and single world government of which every human would be a citizen in what he called a "republic of united individuals."[10] This was probably the most consistent and meaningful cosmopolitan philosophy, but it was also the most unrealistic and unattainable.

As a general rule, cosmopolitanism and its understanding of global citizenship weren't used to denote a distinct model of citizenship. It was (and is) a posture toward politics or an "attitude of open-mindedness and impartiality. A cosmopolitan was someone who was not subservient to a particular religious or political authority, someone who was not biased by particular loyalties or cultural prejudice."[11] Like its ancient Stoic heritage, it's committed to aiding the world outside of one's own nation in charitable work as well as activism designed to promote justice and secure human rights across the world irrespective of borders.

However, some modern variants have reasserted a political cosmopolitanism, albeit one that's much more nuanced and realistic than Cloots's proposals in the eighteenth century. For example, the American political philosopher John Rawls, in his celebrated *The Laws of the Peoples*, lays out a theory for greater unity and therefore a broadened understanding of citizenship for countries with similar governments, sympathies, and morality. It's more international than cosmopolitan in that he recognizes the impossibility of a world-state filled with world citizens, for a world government would essentially be a global tyranny, and there would always be groups competing and fighting for dominance or independence. However, an international order of an increasing number of member states, and therefore citizens, would be able to bring about the disappearance of the great evils of history, such as "unjust war and oppression, religious persecution and the denial of liberty of conscience, starvation and poverty, not to mention genocide and mass murder."[12] The result would be what he calls a realistic (quasi-global) utopia.

Moderate moral and political cosmopolitanism certainly seem attractive. They are, however, not above criticism, for while they might rightly assume the common humanity of all people, they often fail to take seriously the corruption and depravity of humanity. This often leads to other naïvetés of the utopian dreams of cosmopolitanism. Additionally, cosmopolitanism that denies or downplays the republican and liberal models of citizenship very quickly neglects to give back to those from whom the cosmopolitan has in tangible ways benefitted—that is, one's country and fellow citizens—and makes a mess of any rational prioritization of our civic and social loyalties.[13] As the saying goes, "Everyone wants to change the world, but nobody wants to change the toilet paper roll." Even so, the world has been and continues to be globalized. The social, political, and economic borders that set people apart so often in the past are increasingly being altered and reduced. The concerns and insights of cosmopolitanism will remain relevant as nations and their citizens navigate the future.

## Citizenship in the Christian Tradition

The Christian tradition has something of value to say regarding citizenship too. From the beginning, it acknowledged the legitimacy of the political arena: "Render to Caesar the things that are Caesar's," said Jesus when asked a question about taxation (Matthew 22:21). When the Roman official Pontius Pilate asserted his political authority, Jesus responded by acknowledging it; he even added that Pilate's authority had, in a way, been given to him by God: "You would have no authority over me at all unless it had been given you from above" (John 19:11).

The apostle Paul, too, was explicit about the divine origins of government and the prerogative of Christians to accept it. In Romans 13:1–7, he wrote,

> Let every person be subject to the governing authorities. For there is no authority except from God, and those that exist have been instituted by God. Therefore whoever resists the authorities resists what God has appointed, and those who resist will incur judgment. For rulers are not a terror to good conduct, but to bad. Would you have no fear of the one who is in authority? Then do what is good, and you will receive his approval, for he is God's servant for your good. But if you do wrong, be afraid, for he does not bear the sword in vain. For he is the servant of God, an avenger who carries out God's wrath on the wrongdoer. Therefore one must be in subjection, not only to avoid God's wrath but also for the sake of conscience. For because of this you also pay taxes, for the authorities are ministers of God, attending to this very thing. Pay to all what is owed to them: taxes to whom taxes are owed, revenue to whom revenue is owed, respect to whom respect is owed, honor to whom honor is owed.

As a Roman citizen, Paul would even appeal to his right for a fair trial (see Acts 25:11) as a citizen of the Roman city of Tarsus (see Acts 21:39) after he was arrested in Jerusalem.

While the legitimacy of political order—even one that was hostile to Christianity—and the obligations and rights of citizenship in the secular arena are explicitly recognized in the Christian tradition, they're also held in view of another reality of citizenship. The Bible suggests that Christians hold a dual citizenship. They are, of course, citizens of political and secular polities on earth, but they also hold a spiritual citizenship. They are, as Paul put it, "fellow citizens with the saints and members of the household of God" (Ephesians 2:19).

Christians are, thus, creatures and citizens of two polities. The greatest expositor of this concept was Saint Augustine of Hippo (354–430). In his massive twenty-two-book-long *City of God*, the North African bishop asserted that there are two cities—or world cities (cosmopolises)—that simultaneously coexist and are intertwined with each other. One is the city of man. This is the realm of politics. It comprises all the polities of the temporal world and is ordered around worldly things. The other is the city of God. It's the church and is ordered by the love for God and the pursuit of his will. The former has a definite temporal end. The latter might be located in time and space for a time, but after the secular world and its governments reach their appointed end, whenever that may be, it would persist with God for all eternity. The loyalty of Christians, then, is to the city of God. To it, they are obligated; by it, they have rights as coheirs in the Kingdom of God. Only for a time are Christians required to live in the city of man. They may even have temporal rights here. Their loyalty mustn't be divided though. In matters temporal, while they should strive to be good and dutiful citizens, ultimately a Christian is more of a pilgrim anxiously awaiting the greater end of citizenship in God's eternal city.

This could and did lead to a sort of rejection, or at least an ignoring, of the importance of political life for Christians in the centuries that followed, especially in western monasticism. However, debates over the relationship between the temporal world and the eternal community of God did persist through the Middle Ages, with a view of the pope being the final authority on earth and leader of men and women to their eternal destiny in heaven prevailing over other alternatives.

A revision of Augustine's thesis emerged during the Protestant Reformation when Martin Luther (1483–1546) began to assert what's often called the doctrine of the two kingdoms:

> God has established two kinds of government among men. The one is spiritual; it has no sword, but it has the word, by means of which men are to become good and righteous, so that with this righteousness they may attain eternal life. He administers this righteousness through the word, which he has committed to the preachers. The other kind is worldly government, which works through the sword

so that those who do not want to be good and righteous to eternal life may be forced to become good and righteous in the eyes of the world. He administers this righteousness through the sword. And although God will not reward this kind of righteousness with eternal life, nonetheless, he still wishes peace to be maintained among men and rewards them with temporal blessings. . . . Thus God himself is the founder, lord, master, protector, and rewarder of both kinds of righteousness. This is no human ordinance or authority in either, but each is a divine thing entirely.[14]

So as in Augustine, a Christian holds a kind of dual citizenship. But in Luther's view, while participation or citizenship in the temporal realm doesn't serve eternal ends, it does serve God's temporal purpose of establishing and preserving civil righteousness. Luther was careful and always cautioned against confusing the spiritual with the secular. He always strove to make a "precise distinction between . . . secular society and religion"[15] and regarded participation in the former as incumbent upon Christians. The obligation of the Christian citizen in the secular arena, however, wasn't subjectively determined. For Luther, it was linked to and defined by one's vocations (or stations) in life, such as father or daughter, a citizen of the Holy Roman Empire of the German Nation or of the Republic of Florence, a soldier or pastor, and so on. And it must be taken seriously not for the sake of one's righteousness before God but for the maintenance of civil righteousness in human societies.

## Neighbors

While one's vocations determine an individual's activity in civil society, Luther also believed that every Christian has certain obligations to his or her neighbor, not as a matter of politics but as an agent of God on earth. Such obligations are detailed in his explanations of the Ten Commandments from Exodus 20:1–17. For example, the fifth commandment forbids murder. What does this mean? Luther responded, "We should fear and love God so that we do not hurt or harm our neighbor in his body, but help and support him in every physical need." The seventh commandment, not to steal, meant that we should "not take our neighbor's money or possessions, or get them in any dishonest way, but help him to improve and protect his possessions and income." The eighth commandment forbids bearing false witness. What this meant, in Luther's mind, was that we "should fear and love God so that we do not tell lies about our neighbor or, betray him, slander him, or hurt his reputation, but defend, him, speak well of him, and explain everything in the kindest way."[16]

In Christianity, all the commandments "are summed up in this word: 'You shall love your neighbor as yourself'" (Romans 13:9). In view of citizenship, this begs the question: Who's my neighbor? Is it just the person next door or is it the person I rub elbows with as I serve in my various roles as a son or daughter, student, citizen, employee, and so forth? Jesus answered the question with the famous parable of the Good Samaritan found in the Gospel of Luke 10:25–37:

> And behold, a lawyer stood up to put him to the test, saying, "Teacher, what shall I do to inherit eternal life?" He said to him, "What is written in the Law? How do you read it?" And he answered, "You shall love the Lord your God with all your heart and with all your soul and with all your strength and with all your mind, and your neighbor as yourself." And he said to him, "You have answered correctly; do this, and you will live." But he, desiring to justify himself, said to Jesus, "And who is my neighbor?" Jesus replied, "A man was going down from Jerusalem to Jericho, and he fell among robbers, who stripped him and beat him and departed, leaving him half dead. Now by chance a priest was going down that road, and when he saw him he passed by on the other side. So likewise a Levite, when he came to the place and saw him, passed by on the other side. But a Samaritan, as he journeyed, came to where he was, and when he saw him, he had compassion. He went to him and bound up his wounds, pouring on oil and wine. Then he set him on his own animal and brought him to an inn and took care of him. And the next day he took out two denarii and gave them to the innkeeper, saying, 'Take care of him, and whatever more you spend, I will repay you when I come back.' Which of these three, do you think, proved to be a neighbor to the man who fell among the robbers?" He said, "The one who showed him mercy." And Jesus said to him, "You go, and do likewise."

This parable has many applications. The point to be made here is that a neighbor isn't just our fellow citizen who, like the priest, the

Levite, and the man from Jerusalem, is in good standing in our particular polity. Our neighbor is anyone we might encounter from the entire human race. The Samaritan, despised by the citizens of Israel, is the one who demonstrated what it is to be a good neighbor, for he took care of even someone who may have, in other circumstances, hated him.

In the Christian tradition, then, there's room for service to one's nation as a citizen fulfilling various obligations—both political and domestic—and there's the impetus for a moral cosmopolitanism of a sort where the individual is active as the opportunity presents itself to extend care and service to one's fellow humans irrespective of citizenship and nationality.

## Concluding Considerations

There's no singular way to understand citizenship. The three models described previously—republican, liberal, and cosmopolitan—all have their rationale and merits. The republican model is perhaps the most historic and, up until the modern emphasis (perhaps overemphasis) on rights, had the most influence up to and through the American Revolution. The liberal model is likewise a fairly permanent fixture in modern societies, although it's contingent and relative to the polities that define the rights of their constituents. While both are distinct, they can and do work together. Advocates of both would insist that they need to work alongside each other. Despite the abstractedness, the cosmopolitan tradition also compliments the models organized around a distinct polity by tempering overzealous nationalisms and providing the impetus for advancing justice and extending human rights wherever they might gain a foothold. All three could be blended to some degree or another by any citizen of any nation. However, where it's articulated most clearly—and grounded in the objective foundation of God's natural (and special) revelation as a corrective to the ever-changing whims of man—is in the historic Christian tradition.

## Exercises for Reflection and Discussion

1. Write a definition for each model of citizenship discussed in this chapter: republican, liberal, and cosmopolitan. What are the strengths and weaknesses of each model? Are they mutually exclusive or can they be blended together? Is there a benefit to blending them?

2. How does the historic Christian tradition approach citizenship and cosmopolitanism?

3. How do you see these three models of citizenship at work in the country where you hold citizenship? Do these models work well with each other? Is one model emphasized more? Do you agree with that emphasis?

4. Think of your citizenship, whether American or in another country. What are your political rights and obligations? How do you assert your freedoms and fulfill your duties? Talk about this with a friend, relative, or teacher.

5. Think about the various stations and places you work and inhabit. Identify two specific neighbors that you encounter in those places, one who's a citizen of your country and one who isn't. In what ways might you serve those neighbors, now and in the future?

## Notes

1 Thucydides, *History of the Peloponnesian War*, trans. Rex Warner (New York: Penguin, 1954), 145.

2 Thucydides, 147.

3 Aristotle, *Politics*, trans. Ernest Baker (New York: Oxford University Press, 1995), 10.

4 Aristotle, 85.

5 Dominique Leydet, "Citizenship," in *The Stanford Encyclopedia of Philosophy*, fall 2017 edition, ed. Edward N. Zalta, accessed October 10, 2019, https://plato.stanford.edu/archives/fall2017/entries/citizenship/.

6 For the complete text of the Declaration of Independence, see https://www.archives.gov/founding-docs/declaration-transcript.

7 Leydet, "Citizenship."

8 Michael Walzer, "Citizenship," in *Political Innovation and Conceptual Change*, ed. T. Ball, J. Farr, and R. L. Hanson (New York: Cambridge University Press, 1989), 217.

9  Pauline Kleingeld and Eric Brown, "Cosmopolitanism," in *The Stanford Encyclopedia of Philosophy*, fall 2014 edition, ed. Edward N. Zalta, accessed October 10, 2019, https://plato.stanford.edu/archives/fall2014/entries/cosmopolitanism/.

10  Pauline Kleingeld, *Kant and Cosmopolitanism: The Philosophical Ideal of World Citizenship* (New York: Cambridge University Press, 2012), 40.

11  Kleingeld and Brown, "Cosmopolitanism."

12  John Rawls, *The Law of Peoples* (Cambridge, MA: Harvard University Press, 1999), 6–7.

13  On this theme, see Alasdair MacIntyre, "Is Patriotism a Virtue?," in *Theorizing Citizenship*, ed. Ronald Beiner (Albany: State University of New York Press, 1995), 209–28.

14  Martin Luther, "Whether Soldiers, Too, Can Be Saved," in *Luther's Works*, American Edition, 55 vols., ed. Jaroslav Pelikan and Helmut T. Lehmann (Philadelphia: Muehlenberg and Fortress / St. Louis: Concordia, 1955–86), 46:99–100 (hereinafter LW).

15  Luther, "Lectures on Galatians (1535): Chapters 1–4," in LW, 26:7.

16  Martin Luther, *Luther's Small Catechism* (St. Louis: Concordia, 1991), 12–14.

# Living Honorably as a Worker

*Christopher "Kit" Nagel*

## The Virtue of Being Well-Rounded

The term *worker* is a broad heading. Certainly young people, as one chapter in this book talks about, work at their studies. Another chapter talks about the vocations of neighbor and citizen, which naturally also require work. This chapter will move away from the broad vocational heading and carve out a focus on living honorably as a worker in life after university—when, through God's grace, one charts one's own way in the world.

The purpose of this chapter is to offer an approach to navigating the world of work and also to give some guidance for that journey. The perspective offered here is that of a business professor and former corporate manager, but the truths of right and honorable behavior and the goal of living an ethical life of service crosses all disciplines. We'll discuss how to prepare for the future and show that the challenges to living an honorable life aren't dissimilar to those faced in the days of Luther, five hundred years ago.

Let's look down the road to life and career. And let's also presume you defer graduate school for a couple of years and secure a fine entry-level position. After an appropriate time of hard work in the trenches learning and becoming acclimated to an industry (e.g., solar power or health care) or an institution (e.g., US State Department), you move into managing others. Here, though still a worker, you will lead and direct other subordinate workers.

Life's all about preparation, transition, and one's journey. Let's begin with a great quote from "A Sermon on Keeping Children in School," written by the sixteenth-century theological and educational reformer Martin Luther: "I shall say nothing here about the pure pleasure a person gets from having studied. . . . to read all kinds of things, talk and associate with educated people, and travel and do business in foreign lands."[1] Here Luther sees the vocation of student leading to a full life of the mind, pushing broad horizons, and being out and about in the world—not in some cloister or monastery or sitting in a dorm room playing video games. Luther says that students should be prepared to "take their place in the stream of human events."[2] It's interesting that Luther's world view included not only business but also international business. So briefly, let's ask the question: What is business?

There are many misconceptions about the role of business, lots of soap opera stuff. But one can say that businesses are employers, investors, polluters, producers, and purveyors of products like wind turbines, iPhones, and Subarus. A business can be for-profit or a charitable not-for-profit (e.g., Americares or Lutheran Social Services). A business is the accountant who does your taxes, the plumber who unclogs your drain, and the airline that takes you across a continent. And let's not forget the mining companies that provide ore to the steel mills that provide metal to machinery companies that make the milking parlors used by dairy farmers so that needy students can buy their morning "blond venti lattes."

Business affects all our lives, and it's an arena in which most will have an active role. This reality leads to such questions as, How should we prepare ourselves to navigate the mosaic of worker activities? What should be our core values, our guiding lights? How should we lead others by example in right and honorable behavior? Part of the answer, given by those with experience in business, is that the best workers and the best managers are well-rounded, well-traveled, and well-read. Having a narrow world view or silo of knowledge is simply not enough. The globally experienced journalist Thomas Friedman notes the value of such well-roundedness when he says, "Today, more than ever the traditional boundaries between politics, culture, technology, finance, national security, and ecology are disappearing. You often cannot explain one without referring to the others, and you cannot explain the whole without reference to them all. . . . In a world where we are so much more interconnected, the ability to read the connections, and to connect the dots, is the real value added. If you don't see the connections, you won't see the world."[3] From a corporate perspective—and to help students position themselves to be effective workers or, in Luther's words, take their place in the stream of human events—the CEO of Beam-Suntory, Albert Baladi, advises that "companies are increasingly interconnected between geographies and functional expertise. Innovations and big achievements are often borne from the leverage of this interconnectedness, and successful employees are those who thrive in this cross-functional, cross-geographical network. Effective two-way communication, and more specifically emphatic listening, is one of the key enablers. So to prepare students, putting extra emphasis on listening and more broadly communication skills, is a very valuable complement to overseas studies, internships, and social experiences."[4] And in reflecting on his own journey, George Vojta, the former chair of the Board of Governors of the Federal Reserve System, says, "My success came from a generalist background in what I'll call political economy. There is a need for a global perspective and knowledge of other cultures. There is now a move away from 'intense specialization' to a broader concept of leadership and the larger perspective of service to clients and service to society."[5] These are truths that help explain why business faculty so value robust liberal arts, or "core curriculum," programs at universities. In the liberal arts tradition, those who embrace diversity, develop a breadth of knowledge, and are able to connect the dots are then better able to be a bridge between disciplines, peoples, and cultures. In business, this is a huge value added.

Perhaps this is obvious, but knowledge of one's world is fundamental to being well-rounded. Yet in recent years, university faculty see students arriving on campus with increasingly less knowledge about their world. The sad reality is that given a map of the Middle East, only 31 percent of American students are able to identify Israel. When asked to name the United States' largest trading partner, most get it wrong, saying it's China; only 10 percent give the correct answer of Canada.[6] And on civic-mindedness and the vocation of being a citizen, only 26 percent of Americans can name all three branches of government.[7] In some high schools, teachers have even told students they don't actually need to know anything; they just need to be able to find it online. This is silly. As per Friedman's perspective mentioned previously, if one doesn't even know that the dots exist, how can one hope to connect them?

Happily, many students do pursue broad horizons, recognizing that globalization is upon us—a reality that we all must navigate. No great surprise then that in looking to the future, there's a clear need for globally minded workers in both government and business. Mike Eskew, a director of 3M, notes the great shortage of workers who are "global trade literate, sensitive to foreign cultures, conversant in different languages."[8] In any well-run business today, diversity isn't seen as a problem to be managed but a beneficial and competitive asset. One of the author's former students, Stéphane Laroche, is posted in Abuja, Nigeria, with the United States Agency for International Development (USAID). He reports that "in [their] work, colleagues at all echelons come from various corners of our nation and world. Together, when workers and leaders hold diversity and inclusion as foundational values, the organization benefits from the resulting diverse set of ideas. This then leads to innovations that directly help solve problems and so better serve society."[9] Given the previous statements, students should reflect on how best to prepare themselves to be effective and productive workers in the larger world. Students, in becoming workers, should go out with good courage and engage the world, being confident in the biblical admonition that Moses gave to Joshua and the Israelites before they entered into a new land: "[The LORD] will be with you; he will not leave you or forsake you. Do not fear or be dismayed" (Deuteronomy 31:8). We all need to keep our horizons broad and be open to, work with, and enjoy the wonderful diversity of God's peoples (the world is a big place; only 4.4 percent of the world's population lives in the US). However, in sad and ignorant contrast, we see today's politicians build their appeal with a demagogue's design on promoting fear of the foreign, the unfamiliar, and the immigrant. America is thus diminished. In a real-world comment, travel writer Rick Steves notes, "Fear is for people who don't get out very much."[10] And this echoes the view of the nineteenth-century

American humorist Mark Twain: "Travel is fatal to prejudice, big-otry, and narrow-mindedness."[11] So get out there, enjoy Ecuador, befriend an Italian.

## Once Prepared, How Should We Work?

Let's now switch gears from positioning ourselves for life and career and look to the relevance of Luther's writings on the vocation of the worker in both his day and our own. While the main focus of Luther's work is on the redemptive power of the gospel, his extensive writings include commentary on such work and business-related issues as pricing, free markets, cross-border trade, compound inter-est, monopolies, and the role of government. Unpacking all these is beyond the scope of this brief chapter, but Luther's underlying view on our role as workers follows his theologically based approach of *Nächstenliebe* (pronounced neck-sten-leeba). This loosely translates as "love of neighbor," meaning the necessary love and care for those together with us in society, our fellow citizens, our neighbors.

In his Luther biography, Roland Bainton quotes Luther's treatise "On the Freedom of a Christian" to explain this approach: "When God in his sheer mercy and without any merit of mine has given me such unspeakable riches, shall I not then freely, joyously, whole-heartedly, unprompted do everything that I know will please him? I will give myself as a sort of Christ to my neighbor as Christ gave himself for me." Bainton calls this the "epitome of Luther's ethic, that a Christian must be a Christ to his neighbor."[12]

Such *Nächstenliebe* should be our vocational aspiration. Yet we live in a fallen world and must stand strong when others push us to selfishness, greed, prejudice, and yes, the coarsening of daily dis-course. A common example is those who don't discuss or argue an issue on the merits but attack the appearance, intelligence, or ethnic-ity of the person making the argument. Such ad hominem (against a person) attacks should have no role in communal or corporate life, yet sadly, many go down that road.

Since we're called to take our place as workers in the world, we need to prepare ourselves for the challenges we all face to liv-ing an honorable life of *Nächstenliebe*. So it's worthwhile here to give examples of those who've strayed from the honorable path. As noted, the author's discipline is business, so that will be the focus. In reality, most workers are regular folk who strive to live their lives and vocations with decency, take care of their families, and participate in a faith community. American business isn't all about Hollywood-style greedy villains, though there are some. As a cautionary tale, let's take a look at temptation and greedy villains in both Luther's time and ours. We should add that Luther didn't single out business workers as the only ones driven by greed. He condemned greed in members of all classes (*Stände*), and no profession is any greedier than another. Nevertheless, here are examples from the dark side of business.

Luther keenly observed the detrimental effects of market manipulation and monopolies. In his commentary "Trade and Usury," Luther talks of economic coercion when a merchant takes advantage of customers to reap unfair profits—especially the manipulation brought on by monopoly power. His concern remains every bit as valid today as monopolies and market manipulations wreck the beneficial efficiency of free markets. Luther noted that "there are some who buy up the entire supply of certain goods or wares in a country or city in order to have these goods entirely under their own control; they can then fix and raise the price and sell as dear as they like or can. . . . Even the imperial and secular laws forbid this; they call it *monopolia*. . . . For such merchants act as if God's creatures and God's goods were created and given for them alone, as if they could take them from others and set on them whatever price they chose."[13] While monopolies in Luther's time were illegal, the laws weren't enforced against the great trading houses. A case study from Luther's time is the Augsburg family of the Fuggers, a major banking house that held monopolies in mining, commerce, and finance. With no legal limitations or competitive constraints from what Luther called the common market (*gemein markt*), the Fuggers amassed a huge fortune. Resonating with the lamentable state of American politics today, the Fuggers made enormous cash outlays that secured the imperial election of Emperor Charles V. The quid pro quo (something for something) ensured that the authorities wouldn't move against the elite Fuggers or limit their monopoly power.

Tied to this case, and as the Luther story always includes his strident opposition to the sale of Papal Indulgences, we should also note the Fuggers's role in this commercial transaction. It gets ugly. In 1517, Albert of Brandenburg wanted to be the archbishop of Mainz, which would make him an important fellow, the primate of all Germany. Knowing he'd need to pay Rome a huge sum to buy the office, he retained the Fugger banking house to negotiate with Pope Leo X (not coincidentally, the Fuggers already held a monopoly on papal finances in Germany). The pontiff and the Fuggers settled on a figure of ten thousand ducats, and Albert had to pay Leo up front before receiving the papal appointment. He borrowed the ducats from the Fuggers. To enable Albert to recoup the huge cost, Leo granted him an eight-year privilege to sell Papal Indulgences. The deal stipulated that beyond the ten thousand ducats already received by the pope, half of the Indulgence revenues would go to Leo for building the new St. Peter's Basilica in Vatican City, the other half going to the Fuggers to service the loan and as added compensation for handling the transaction.

Luther was disgusted with the connivance of the secular, political, and religious powers. He was surely including the Fuggers when, in the "Large Catechism," he condemned the "great, powerful arch-thieves with whom lords and princes consort and who daily plunder not just a city or two, but all Germany" and called the pope in Rome the "head and chief protector of all thieves."[14] Harsh words for a harsh, corrupt, and abusive time. However, Luther's underlying social concern—which was motivated by both reason's natural law of fairness and faith's love toward one's neighbor in response to Christ's love—remains instructive. Pricing and trade should be market-driven and, at the same time, not exploitive or coercive. Freely fluctuating prices in a competitive marketplace are a necessary and beneficial underpinning of a market economy. The role of business and trade can and should be to improve the quality of life in society. Both parties, the buyer and the seller, should gain from an exchange—perhaps not in some elegant theoretical balance, but trade should lead to mutual benefit.

In his "Large Catechism," Luther comments on the biblical commandment "You shall not steal" (see Exodus 20:15). He gives a harsh and bombastic admonition to workers that theft is taking advantage of our neighbors in any sort of dealings that result in loss to them. . . . taking advantage of someone in the market . . . wherever business is transacted and money is exchanged for goods or services. . . . Furthermore, at the market and in everyday business the same fraud prevails in full power in force. One person openly cheats another with defective merchandise, false weights and measurements, and counterfeit coins, and takes advantage of the other by deception and sharp practices and crafty dealings. Or again, one swindles another in a trade and deliberately fleeces, skins, and torments him. Who can even describe or imagine it all? In short, thievery is the most common craft and the largest guild on earth. If we look at the whole of the world in all its situations, it is nothing but a big, wide stable full of great thieves.[15]

Luther also calls many merchants *Stuhlräuber* (seated thieves). For "far from being picklocks and sneak thieves who pilfer the cash box, they sit in their chairs and are known as great lords and honorable, upstanding citizens, while they rob and steal under the cloak of legality. . . . In short, this is the way of the world." Luther then adds for us a core ethic: "Let all people know, then, that it is their duty, on pain of God's displeasure, not to harm their neighbors, to take advantage of them, or to defraud them by any faithless or underhanded business transaction. Much more than that, they are also obligated faithfully to protect their neighbors' property and to promote and further their interests, especially when they get money, wages, and provisions for doing so."[16] Moving now to our world today, we can readily connect Luther's admonition against "sharp practices and crafty dealings" with the private-sector-induced market meltdown of 2008. This was a time when many US financial houses succumbed to avarice and greed, knowing full well that what they did was unsustainable. Abusing a trusted role in society, many bankers and financiers—what Luther would call "greedy-bloated fellows" (*geizige Blasen*)—grew recklessly wealthy. Their behavior became so profitable that, while driving the economy into ruin, financial sector profits spiked to over 40 percent of the profits in the *entire* US economy. This compares to the financial sector's average share of profits from 1970 to 2000 of 20.2 percent.[17] (Does anyone want to argue that financial services contribute 40 percent of the well-being of our country?) Key poster children of this nonsense are the managers at the failed Lehman Brothers. They absolutely knew their actions were dangerous and added risk not only to their company but to society at large. Yet the *geizige Blasen* would "get theirs." Their attitude was, "Let's get our cash out, park it in T-Bills, and let the thing crash." In Lehman, this was called IBG-YBG (I'll be gone, and you'll be gone). No kidding. When a middle-level manager approached his boss with a concern that what the firm was doing was wrong and unsustainable, the response was, "Don't worry, IBG-YBG." The firm was led by Richard Fuld, who, while flying his company into failure and helping crater the US economy, "got his" by taking out earnings of $71.9 million. Tragically for the country, greed and avarice prevailed with a pathetic lack of concern for *Nächstenliebe*. They had lost their ethical rudder, turning their backs on the foundational guideposts that Jesus gave to all people, including the wealthy: "Do not steal, Do not bear false witness, Do not defraud" (Mark 10:19).

In some ways, we haven't progressed much since Luther looked out at his world. An article in the *Economist* magazine summarizes where we stand today: "During the financial crisis, governments used oceans of public money to rescue banks from the consequences of their own folly and greed. Bankers quickly went back to paying themselves fat bonuses. Inequality is growing in many countries. Plutocrats wax richer as the middle class is squeezed and the poor are trodden underfoot. Hedge-fund moguls and casino kings spend fortunes to sway American elections—and the Supreme Court tells them to carry on spending."[18] Here the *Economist* is alluding to conservative mogul Sheldon Adelson who said he was willing to spend $100 million to affect a presidential outcome. On "inequality," the CEOs of the largest US firms earn annually an average of $15 million, nearly three hundred times more than a typical worker (forty years ago, the ratio was 26:1).[19] (Does anyone want to argue that one person's work is worth three centuries of work by another?) The "Supreme Court" reference is the court's ruling in the Citizens United case that "money equals speech" or, as with the Fuggers, money talks. The late Republican senator John McCain called this the "worst decision by the Supreme Court in the twenty-first century; uninformed, arrogant, naive."[20] One can almost hear Luther again rising to assail the "great, powerful archthieves with whom lords and princes consort and who daily plunder not just a city or two, but all Germany."

## Decide Where You Stand

So where do we go from here and how can we benefit from the caring perspective of the great reformer? Clearly we all need to carry Luther's theologically rooted perspective and understanding of ethical moorings in these times of economic challenge and transition. Luther's legacy is an emphasis that our focus as workers, as economic agents, shouldn't be a simple impersonal calculus. It should be one that incorporates fairness to others as a guide and constraint and does much more than simply what's legal. Markets and legalities shouldn't have the final say in determining our actions or our neighbor's welfare. So decide who you are; decide where you stand.

We can close with a quote and a hymn. Bainton's great Luther biography offers this summary of a worker's role: "In the realm of economics [Luther] considered less [the] abstract laws of supply and demand than the personal relations of buyer and seller, debtor and creditor."[21] The appropriate admonition for young people—society's rising cohort of workers and managers—from this neighbor-centered approach to work is twofold. Consider your impact on others with whom you will deal. And follow Luther's *Nächstenliebe*, the necessary love and care for those together with you in society—your fellow citizens and neighbors. Your neighbor's needs and Christ's love call you to work this way. So Frank von Christierson's hymn "As Saints of Old" directs us to sing,

> A world in need now summons us to labor, love, and give;
> To make our life an offering to God, that all may live. . . .
> O God, who gave yourself to us in Jesus Christ your Son,
> Teach us to give ourselves each day until life's work is done.[22]

## Exercises for Reflection and Discussion

1. Why does the author stress that "life is all about preparation, transition, and one's journey"?

2. What do you think the purpose of work is? How do others around you—family, peers, or the media—define work?

3. The prophets of the Old Testament also addressed ethics in economics. Read Amos 8:4-6 and Micah 6:9-11. How do the concepts of fairness and *Nächstenliebe* (love of neighbor) discussed in this chapter help explain why Amos and Micah condemn certain business practices in ancient Israel? Finally, how does Leviticus 19:9-10, 13, 19, 35-36 define virtuous business practices? Give an example of how that would apply today.

4. This chapter focuses on how to act in work. Let's also consider what your work vocations could be. To do this, draw a large diagram on a piece of paper that looks like this.

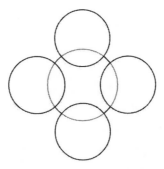

In one outer circle, list the God-given gifts you have—your talents and personality traits. In another circle, list what you like to do, what you're interested in. In another circle, identify the beliefs and virtues (or values) that you hold to be true, good, and beautiful in life. In the final outer circle, note what needs you see around you. That is, what help do other people need to secure or to improve their welfare in life? In the center circle, write down some work vocations that connect your gifts, interests, and beliefs together with serving the needs of others. Under the diagram, plot out the education or experiences you'll need to be prepared to be called by an employer to serve in those work vocations. Share your work vocation diagram and plan with your parents, siblings, friends, or mentors and invite their feedback.

## Notes

1  Martin Luther, "A Sermon on Keeping Children in School," in *Luther's Works*, American Edition, 55 vols., ed. Jaroslav Pelikan and Helmut T. Lehmann (Philadelphia: Muehlenberg and Fortress / St. Louis: Concordia, 1955–86), 46:243 (hereinafter LW).

2  Luther, "To the Councilmen of All Cities in Germany That They Establish and Maintain Christian Schools," in LW, 45:369.

3  Thomas Friedman, *The Lexus and the Olive Tree* (New York: Anchor Books, 2000), 20.

4  The author is grateful for the generous assistance of Albert Baladi, CEO, Beam Suntory.

5  The author is grateful for the generous assistance of George Vojta, vice chair, Bankers Trust.

6  "What College-Aged Students Know about the World: A Survey of Global Literacy," Council on Foreign Relations and National Geographic, September 2016, accessed July 11, 2019, https://www.cfr.org/content/newsletter/files/CFR_NatGeo_ASurveyonGlobalLiteracy.pdf.

7  "Americans Are Poorly Informed about Basic Constitutional Provisions," Annenberg Public Policy Center, September 12, 2017, accessed July 11, 2019, https://www.annenbergpublicpolicycenter.org/americans-are -poorly-informed-about-basic-constitutional-provisions/.

8  Quoted in Claudia Wallis and Sonja Steptoe, "How to Bring Our Schools Out of the 20th Century," *TIME*, December 9, 2006, accessed July 11, 2019, http://content.time.com/time/nation/article/0,8599,1568429,00 .html.

9  The author is grateful for the generous assistance of Stéphane Laroche, foreign service officer, USAID, and Concordia College New York alum.

10  Quoted in Sam Anderson, "Rick Steves Wants to Save the World, One Vacation at a Time," *New York Times*, March 20, 2019, accessed July 11, 2019, https://www.nytimes.com/interactive/2019/03/20/magazine/rick -steves-travel-world.html.

11  Mark Twain (Samuel L. Clemens), *The Innocents Abroad or The New Pilgrim's Progress* (1869; repr., Hertfordshire: Wordsworth Editions, 2010), 427.

12  Roland H. Bainton, *Here I Stand: A Life of Martin Luther* (Peabody, MA: Hendrickson, 2010), 230–31.

13  Luther, "Trade and Usury," in LW, 45:262.

14  Martin Luther, "Large Catechism," in *The Book of Concord*, ed. Robert Kolb and Timothy J. Wengert (Minneapolis: Fortress, 2000), 417 (230).

15  Luther, 416–17 (224, 227–29).

16  Luther, 417 (229, 231, 233).

17  US Department of Commerce, Bureau of Economic Analysis, Corporate Profits by Industry, accessed July 11, 2019, https://www.bea.gov/data/income-saving/corporate-profits.

18  Schumpeter, "The Transience of Power," *Economist*, March 16, 2013, 70.

19  Steven Brill, "My Generation Was Supposed to Level America's Playing Field. Instead, We Rigged It for Ourselves," *TIME*, May 28, 2018, 35.

20  John McCain, interview with David Gregory, *Meet the Press*, NBC, June 7, 2012.

21  Bainton, *Here I Stand*, 236.

22  Frank von Christierson, "As Saints of Old" (1961), in *Lutheran Book of Worship* (Minneapolis: Augsburg Fortress, 2006), 404.

# Hearing the Call to Care for Nature

*Sarah L. Karam*

## Vocation of Caretaker of Nature

Although it may be easy to see yourself living out many of the other vocations in this book, you may never have thought about being personally called to care for nature. Our culture's common definition of vocation is aligned with work, and our Christian love and service tend to focus on our fellow humans. Culturally, caring for nature is integrated into systems of beliefs about religion, politics, and society, and it's therefore a social movement rather than an individual calling. You might identify caring for nature as a lifestyle choice rather than a spiritual vocation you're compelled to carry out. Those of us with relative wealth and its attendant technology don't even have to think about obtaining food and water, let alone recognize that natural resources make up our houses, cell phones, and even the air we breathe. What we do hear about nature in the media often sounds apocalyptic—fires, tornados, global warming, bee colony collapse—as if the end is imminent and there's nothing we can do to stop it. As such, caring for nature may seem less personal, relational, and righteous than other callings, or may even be overlooked entirely.

Contrary to this perspective, caring for nature is exactly what God created us to do. The very first vocation God called humans to do in Genesis 1:26–28 was to care for nature:

> Then God said, "Let us make man in our image, after our likeness. And let them have dominion over the fish of the sea and over the

birds of the heavens and over the livestock and over all the earth and over every creeping thing that creeps on the earth."

So God created man in his own image,

in the image of God he created him;

male and female he created them.

And God blessed them. And God said to them, "Be fruitful and multiply and fill the earth and subdue it, and have dominion over the fish of the sea and over the birds of the heavens and over every living thing that moves on the earth."

This translation uses the word *dominion* for the Hebrew word *radah*, which may be among the most debated words in the Bible (and, lucky for me being a nonexpert on the topic, outside the scope of this chapter). A very general definition might be "having the right and responsibility to govern the rest of nature." The exact nature of this governing isn't specified but has been interpreted to mean benevolently, as God who created them would do.[1] In Genesis 2:7–15, humans are created out of the dust of the earth and put "in the garden of Eden to work it and keep it." Here the word *work* for the Hebrew word *avad* might be translated as "till" or "serve," often used to refer to the service a servant gives a master in the Old Testament. The word *keep* for *shamar* emphasizes active protection from harm. Both of these words are also frequently used in the sacred context of Levites carrying out their tabernacle duties, including serving God and keeping the tabernacle from harm.[2] Together, Genesis 1 and 2 have been interpreted by many biblical scholars as calling humans to the sacred vocation of serving and protecting nature as God's representatives on earth.

In this chapter, I want you to consider how to hear the call to this vocation and what it might look like for you to serve nature personally in your current culture and context. Consider nature as your neighbor. Rather than being told exactly what a good caretaker of nature should do, you'll be asked to consider how philosophical beliefs and life experiences shape your relationship with nature and then invited to imagine how to strengthen that relationship. Hear God's call to fulfill this vocation for the glory of God and the love of your neighbor.

## God Has an Ongoing Relationship with Nature

> In the beginning, God created the heavens and the earth. The earth was without form and void, and darkness was over the face of the deep. And the Spirit of God was hovering over the face of the waters. And God said, "Let there be light," and there was light. And God saw that the light was good. (Genesis 1:1–4)

In Judeo-Christian theology, God created the universe and all that's in it, humanity included, calling order out of chaos. Each day brought creation that was good, and after the sixth day, God declared all that he had created to be "very good" (Genesis 1:31). He called humans to "be fruitful and multiply" (Genesis 1:28) and thus share in this creative work, as do fish and birds (see Genesis 1:22). And then, the Fall—humans sinned and God cursed the serpent, man, and the ground (see Genesis 3:14–19)—resulted in disorder for all he had created, not just Adam and Eve. Human sin also resulted in God flooding the earth to the detriment of every part of it. God saved nature through Noah, his family, and the animals protected on the ark and made a covenant with all living creatures to never again destroy the earth despite humanity's ongoing sin (see Genesis 9:8–17).

We often talk about God's creation incompletely, in the past tense, limiting it to "in the beginning," as if God created and now just sits and watches what unfolds from a distance. In contrast to this popular image, Christians believe in a living God who has a personal, ongoing relationship as Creator and Savior to his creation, sustaining it and dying to reconcile all of it through Jesus Christ (see Colossians 1:16–20). Christ links redemption to creation as one divine act, restoring *all* of creation to God's predetermined will and eternal purpose, from the way it is to the way it ought to be. Until the re-creation of a new heaven and new earth with Christ's second coming, we assist in this creative and redemptive work as God works through us to serve our neighbors.

## The Philosophical Nature of Creation and Vocation

You may have noticed a switch in terminology from *nature* to *creation*. That minor change focuses attention on a creator rather than only that which we observe to exist; it takes the discussion from the mundane to the cosmic. Depending on religious beliefs and cultural background, some readers may have felt comfortable with that switch, while others may have bristled at the presumed metaphysics behind the distinction. Then the moral declaration that creation was "good," more so "very good," brought values into consideration.

Due to the terminology and our cultural context, we're aware that my description of God's relationship with nature comes from a particular world view, a Christian one with origins tracing back to early Christian theologians as well as ancient Greek philosophers. Whether this world view is right or wrong in the grand scheme of reality, it has had a huge influence on Western culture. Consider your answers to these questions: Do you think there's a beginning and end to life and the universe? Is the future determined by the past? Are you a separate being or part of a larger collective? Is certainty possible? Do you think objective truth is found outside of yourself? Is there a purpose? Are values absolute? How do you know any of these things?

Humans have wrestled with these kinds of philosophical questions about the fundamental aspects of reality for millennia, with different answers from individuals in different cultures at different times. The history of the vocation concept itself illuminates the dynamic nature of human understanding shifting with world view in the context of culture. In his 2005 book *Calling*, American theologian William Placher traces four broad shifts in Christian understanding of vocation:

1. The early church faced persecution, and so following Christ was vocation itself. Philosophically, dualistic thinking set a high, perfect, sacred life against a low, acceptable, secular life.
2. After Constantine converted to Christianity, Christianity was culturally advantageous, and some Christians turned to monastic self-denial on a mission to reform a secularizing church. There was virtue in freely choosing a life of

suffering for Christ through a contemplative life (high) versus a life of fighting as a noble or, even worse, a life of work (low).

3. In the Reformation, Martin Luther proclaimed the "priesthood of all believers" (see 1 Peter 2:4–10), recognizing all callings as sacred (no more high and low) because no human could contribute anything of value to his or her salvation. Instead, all callings are justified before God by grace through faith in Christ (see Ephesians 2:8–10). Good works were now done for the good of the neighbor, glorifying God. John Calvin's view of work as a sign of God's grace working in the life of a believer further developed work as a spiritual activity, leading to a Protestant work ethic and reduction of the meaning of vocation to economic work.

4. In the current post-Christian age, Placher finds vocation to be more aligned with self-expression than economic work. As the culture became more secular, work was divorced from the primary call to glorify God. Work became a fulfilling end in itself, leading to difficulty identifying work as a calling from God into vocation.[3]

Each of these incarnations embodies meaningful aspects of God's calling to humans, but none captures the complete fullness. Each shift was countercultural against a dominant world view that idolized some aspect of life, and thus each was radical in light of a sinful nature. Placher's proposal of an ongoing shift away from centering vocation on economic labor seems like an opening to reevaluate how we conceive vocation, including what the work of vocation is and whom it serves. The vocation of caring for nature provides a means for reframing the answers to these questions today.

## Vocation Is Rooted in Personal Relationships

The purpose of every vocation is to love and serve our neighbors. We aren't called to love and serve *everyone* (and good luck trying to do so with anything but platitudes) but specifically "You shall love your neighbor as yourself" (Matthew 22:39). Every vocation has its particular neighbors whom God specifically places in our lives. These neighbors may be in close, special relationships with us (e.g., a friend) or in informal, temporary relationships (e.g., a customer at work), but they all are connected to us personally. It may seem obvious who your neighbors are. There are probably some specific people with specific needs who come to mind. It's clear that *humans* are potential neighbors (even if we sometimes don't want to admit it, like the priest or Levite in the Good Samaritan parable in Luke 10:25–37), but can neighbors be other kinds of things? If you accept that God is continually engaged in creating, sustaining, and reconciling all of creation, it seems worthwhile to consider the possibility. Since nature encompasses more than humanity, it might take this kind of reimagining of the neighbor concept to fulfill the vocation of caring for nature.

Here are a few questions to spark your thinking: Is the family pet a neighbor who can be loved and served? Is grass growing in a nearby park? Are the microbes in your gut? What about the moon and stars? A mountain? The *Mona Lisa*? Fossil fuels? Rhomb porphyry rocks in Norway? Your cell phone? Satellites in space? All these are things that some people might profess to love (and perhaps even serve), but my guess is that a willingness to call them *neighbors* would vary among the people reading this book. Some of that variation might be due to the differing relationships people can have with these things. Many people have pets and closely love and serve them as members of the family. Some pets even seem to reciprocate in these relationships (dogs are man's best friend!). I'm guessing there are many fewer people who have that kind of relationship with rhomb porphyry, or have even heard of it, perhaps because friend-like relationships are less likely, since rocks don't interact with us in a human-like way. Despite this same limitation, the night sky seems to call many humans to get to know the constellations and spend time with them, reciprocating with awesome feelings of wonder. Perhaps to your dismay, we depend heavily on fossil fuels and technology and spend lots of time with them (not all relationships are positive). Akin to social relationships between humans, each individual member of nature is unique, as is each relationship in the network of relationships forming the whole.

## You Have a Relationship with Nature

At the most basic level, there's no way in which you're not connected to the earth. You arose from it, you rely on it to sustain your life, and you'll go back to it in death. This is a sacred relationship for Christians because God created humans—along with land animals and birds—out of the dust of the earth (see Genesis 2:7, 19) and gave them food to eat from the earth (see Genesis 1:29–30). As Genesis 3:19 puts it,

> By the sweat of your face
>   you shall eat bread,
> till you return to the ground,
>   for out of it you were taken;
> for you are dust,
>   and to dust you shall return.

All humans depend on nature for food to eat, air to breathe, water to drink, fuels for transportation and heating, and materials to make houses, cars, and every other consumer good. These could be thought of as economic relationships. Tiny molecules are constantly being taken into your body, transformed, and released to be taken up into another body. These are chemical relationships. Your body acclimates as temperatures change, as new synapses form in your brain when you learn to catch a fish, and as you sleep at night. These are physiological relationships. Humans live together in groups and keep pets for companionship. These are social relationships. Eating food means you're a predator feeding on prey, harvesting parts from another organism or even killing it. This is an ecological relationship. You're called into relationships with other entities in nature by the physicality of your body. In this way, humans are members of ecosystems just like all other organisms, interdependent with other entities in nature.

You also have thoughts and feelings about nature, a relationship between your mind and nature. Science purports a "thinking" relationship with nature, using observation and reasoning to explain the observable, whereas art is associated with a "feeling" nature, an experiential relationship with beauty and the sublime. Both rely on sensing the details of nature that might otherwise pass by unknown, but the quality of the sensing seems different. In her Pulitzer Prize–winning book, *Pilgrim at Tinker Creek*, American writer Annie Dillard contrasts the "thinking" and "feeling" ways of seeing using an analogy of walking with and without a camera: "When I walk with a camera I walk from shot to shot, reading the light on a calibrated meter. When I walk without a camera, my own shutter opens, and the moment's light prints on my own silver gut. When I see this second way I am above all an unscrupulous observer."[4] Even if you're not a scientist or an artist in your professional vocation and perhaps can't distinguish between different species of ants or detect all the elements in the composition of a landscape, you can't help but sense the external world and think about it.

The relationships so far have probably sounded entirely too positive given the current narrative about the effects of humans on nature. In all humanity—the more than seven billion humans currently on earth, let alone the ones who preceded us—the collective relationship with nature takes on an almost unfathomable scale and magnitude. It appears that no place on the surface of the earth is unaffected by the human species. Our relationship with nature even extends to Mars, out of our universe, and further into the cosmos! Atmospheric chemist and Nobel laureate Paul Crutzen popularized the term *Anthropocene* to describe the current geologic age because he believes humans may now have a larger effect on nature than other natural processes do.[5] Whether this is an accurate analysis is debated, but you're probably aware of many worldwide effects of humans: depletion of resources, pollution, alteration of biogeochemical cycles, climate change, and mass destruction of plants, animals, and their habitats. On the other hand, there are social movements toward environmental protection, sustainability, remediation, and restoration that seek to rebuild a good relationship between humans and nature. Even if you don't personally condone or directly participate in any of these activities, you're indirectly involved by belonging to a culture that propagates them. Each individual human and organism is part of a complex network of relationships, and therefore the well-being and survival of all are interconnected.

## The Nature of Nature

Your relationship with nature is influenced by your world view, a framework of the particular ideas and beliefs through which you perceive, interpret, and interact with the world. What is nature? How do humans relate to it? These are questions that isolate parts of a world view underlying the idea of caring for nature. To address these questions, this book starts from a philosophical bent holding revelation from God as a valid way of knowing truth, rather than ending with a conclusive answer showing this to be true. Humans hold to axioms that have a certain internal consistency, can be explored philosophically and logically, and are the beginning of our understanding rather than the final answer. As such, I can't give a singular answer to these questions that will satisfy all readers, and likewise, I can't compel you to share in my understanding of the vocation of caring for nature. Instead, I'll outline a couple of possible world views about the fundamental nature of nature and of humanity so you can recognize elements of your world view in these possibilities and consider the implications for loving and serving nature.

Western understandings of nature, which tend to ascribe meanings to nature as an essence, inherent force, and the material itself, can be traced from the ancient Greeks. The word *nature* comes from the Latin word *natura*, meaning "birth." As weird as it may seem, the idea that there was a reality unto itself, separate from the gods and detectable by humans, had to be invented. As with any invention, there have been many creative tweaks, imitations, extensions, and reinventions that have led to the complex, multifaceted, sometimes contradictory axioms we hold today.

In ancient Greece, one way nature was conceptualized was as a personified force of a mother that gives life—Mother Nature, Gaia, a goddess in an eternal process of birth. This understanding was imbued not only with the idea of order in the universe governed by natural law but also with the sacred. A view of nature as infused with the divine is found in many cultures, even if the particular nature of the supernatural and its presence in the world differs (e.g., God as Creator versus God as nature). Moses, Jesus, Mohammed, and Black Elk had revelations while isolated in the wilderness, as did the atheist hippies I knew growing up near Santa Cruz. Nature can provoke awe and reverence of the underlying unity in all things. Many eastern philosophies share a vision of the divine literally dwelling within nature, and thus also within humans; rather than looking outward to find God, an individual might look inward to become aware of one's union with God.

A contrasting Christian view of God as Creator and sustainer of nature meant one could look to nature as a source of revelation about the Creator and the created. This understanding of nature as sacred revelation is exemplified by Saint Francis of Assisi (1182–1226). As one story goes, Francis obeyed the Great Commission of Matthew 28:18–20 by going and preaching sermons to birds and flowers, calling them to praise and serve God. In another, he held a waterfowl in his hand and went into ecstasy. In still another, he would call a cricket who lived in his cell to him, she would come, he would command her to sing praises to God, and they would join in singing together. These stories, whether truth or myth, point toward his view of nature as a brother in Christ: "It was not only sentient creatures whom Saint Francis addressed as his sisters: the sun, the moon, wind, fire, all were brothers and sisters to him. His contemporaries described him as taking 'inward and outward delight in almost every creature, and when he handled or looked at them his spirit seemed to be in heaven rather than on earth.' This delight extended to water, rocks, flowers, and trees. This is a description of a person in a state of religious ecstasy, deeply moved by a feeling of oneness with all of nature."[6] If nature is considered sacred because it has been made by God and thus reveals certain truths about its Creator, it makes sense that the ordinary could be perceived as extraordinary in a mystical, affective-oriented relationship between man and nature, and extending through it to God.

Whereas Francis felt a relationship of unity with nature, others conceptualize nature as something entirely separate from humanity, with the dualism of human versus nature akin to that of mind versus body. For American culture, this is highly influential through the wilderness concept, which contrasts nature as the "raw material out of which man has hammered the artifact called civilization," as conservationist Aldo Leopold, in 1949, put it in *A Sand County Almanac*.[7] Wilderness is conceived as including desert, mountains, wildlife, and all the other things that humans have explored but somehow never altered into our own.

Human perception of the wilderness as good versus bad varies. For the first one hundred years the US existed, wilderness started beyond the frontier and was slowly transformed into civilization as settlers moved west. Some settlers described the wilderness with language reminiscent of the exile of the Israelites wandering in the desert: "savage," "desolate," and "barren."[8] It was mankind daily against what the nineteenth-century naturalist Charles Darwin described as the "hostile forces of nature" that inhibit survival in a Malthusian "struggle for existence."[9] Nature includes wildfires, floods, predators, and all manners of things that humans sought to control. Nature was to be subjugated and civilized (and, tragically, the native peoples also with the rest of the wild).

As the frontier was closing in the mid-nineteenth century, there was a shift from fearful awe of nature to wondrous awe of the sublime, echoing the sacred. Nature was a place where one might glimpse the face of God. Rather than civilizing nature, the focus became conservation of the remaining wilderness. The philosopher Henry David Thoreau exemplified this ethos, saying, "In Wildness is the preservation of the World,"[10] and even explicitly calling for all townships to have "a park, or rather a primitive forest, of five hundred or a thousand acres, where a stick should never be cut for fuel, a common possession forever, for instruction and recreation."[11] The conservation movement resulted in national and state park systems designed to protect natural wonders (albeit not in such a way that prevents all human impact). In the *Wilderness Act*, approved in 1964, Howard Zahniser stated, "A wilderness, in contrast with those areas where man and his own works dominate the landscape, is hereby recognized as an area where the earth and its community of life are untrammeled by man, where man himself is a visitor who does not remain."[12] Notice the definition puts wilderness as an original state of nature that humans can only visit and not live in. Nature primarily exists for its own sake, with humans encroaching on it and thus also able to preserve it. To date, a little more than 1 percent of land in the US has been set aside for preservation purposes in nature reserves, wilderness areas, and national parks and monuments.[13]

Since the conservation movement started, the human population has continued to exponentially increase and concentrate into larger cities, resulting in less wilderness land and an increased physical distance from it to the average person. In the US, census records indicate that about 5.1 percent of Americans lived in urban areas by 1790, 25.7 percent by 1870, 51.2 percent by 1920, and 75.2 percent by 1990.[14] There has been a corresponding documented decline in our cultural engagement with nature, evidenced by decreased national park attendance;[15] fewer nature words featured in popular books, songs, and movies;[16] and kids more able to identify Pokémon than common wildlife types.[17] This has been proximally attributed to humans spending more time indoors (anecdotally, everyone over the age of thirty remembers playing outside, unsupervised and free, all summer long, or at least a lot more often than kids these days seem to). The journalist Richard Louv describes this alienation as transforming the entire culture from one generation to the next: "For a new generation, nature is more abstraction than reality. Increasingly, nature is something to watch, to consume, to wear—to ignore."[18] Paradoxically, this alienation seems to be occurring alongside a greater awareness of environmental issues caused by humans. In this image, humans not only intrude on nature but destroy it. Nature is in need of restoration to its historical state. However, the "real" historical state, the true nature, is outside our human perception. At best it is arbitrarily defined by incomplete memories interacting with our current longings and desires.

There are not only common themes in the previous sketches but also elements that are in direct opposition to each other: unity versus separation of God, humans, and nature from each other; nature as a singular entity versus composed of relationships between individual members; humans as essential or accidental to nature; human awe and fear versus wonder of nature; the economic, biological, or philosophical value of nature; and nature as something to be subjugated, preserved, or restored by humans.

All of these resonate for me personally in some way, but they resonate incompletely. My paradigm of nature is dynamic, shifting in different contexts. As an ecologist studying nature (i.e., as a scientist), I start from a methodological position that the existence of a natural world is independent of the supernatural. I hold this view in tension with my Christian understanding of God present in all of creation. When backpacking in the wilderness, I recognize the precariousness of life outside of civilization, but when I experience a wildfire on the dry California hills in my backyard, I also see the precariousness of civilization itself given nature. My understanding of nature is largely dependent on my experiences and culture, as is yours.

## Call of the Wild

> Deep in the forest a call was sounding, and as often as he heard this call, mysteriously thrilling and luring, he felt compelled to turn his back upon the fire and the beaten earth around it, and to plunge into the forest, and on and on, he knew not where or why; nor did he wonder where or why, the call sounding imperiously, deep in the forest. (*The Call of the Wild*)

In the classic novel *The Call of the Wild*, published in 1903, Jack London wrote about a call of the wild as an internal desire to embrace nature and return to a wild state.[19] In the novel, the protagonist is a dog, albeit one with human-like thinking and behavior, who becomes progressively less civilized as he experiences the harsh environment of Alaska and the social competition of service as a sled dog. Some humans, such as Chris McCandless documented by Jon Krakauer in *Into the Wild*, choose to follow the call of nature over the call of civilized society. This kind of call seems to come from within the individual and is expressed as an emotional desire. It's counter-cultural to follow through with this desire. Explorers are lauded as bold, and perhaps foolhardy. Chris McCandless died alone in an abandoned bus in the wilderness of Alaska.

In contrast to this call from the human nature within, the Christian understanding of vocation is that God is calling us, and in response, we take up the cross and serve our neighbor. At its root, Christian vocation doesn't emanate from you. It's not solely about pursuing happiness, making good choices, or pursuing goals, although these can be a part of loving ourselves. Sometimes you might be called to do something you wouldn't choose or didn't expect. Considering that there's a scriptural foundation for the call to care for nature, it's worth considering whether God is calling you personally to do so. You might be literally compelled by the Holy Spirit into vocation, or you might think or feel you're being called. How can you discern that call?

As rational beings, we can think critically about what we experience and know. A particular question that might help is the interrogative *cui bono*. It's a Latin phrase that means "Who stands to gain?" If we're called, it should be our neighbor. For example, if I lower my energy consumption because it lowers my utility bill, but it also helps reduce energy demands and thus fossil fuel use, is that vocation? Vocation doesn't mean that I can't benefit from my actions, for I can love myself as implied in God's second great command (see Matthew 22:36–40). Yet the self isn't wholly the focus. In the case of energy consumption, trying to identify the neighbors requires further thought. In addition to fellow humans, there are nonhuman neighbors affected by such an action that don't look like us, don't speak the same language we do, and might not even reside in the same place as us (fossil fuels are a global business). To get to know these other neighbors, it might take thinking through the world in terms of interconnected systems, what I'll call an "ecological imagination" in imitation of the "sociological imagination" coined by American sociologist C. Wright Mills.

The phrase *sociological imagination* refers to an ability to see how things interact and influence each other in society. Rather than relying solely on our limited experiences to guide our understanding of the social world, the sociological imagination asks individuals to see that the events in the personal life are related to events in society and that personal challenges are related to large social issues. We have some degree of influence on personal matters (e.g., a person who consumes resources in excess of individual need is gluttonous), but when overconsumption is the status quo for most Americans, our personal choice is made in the context of a larger social issue. According to the sociological imagination, these larger social issues are rooted in society, beyond our personal control and the self. In a capitalist society, consumerism shapes our desires and behaviors to fit in with the rest of society. Resource limitation also prohibits meeting these desires for everyone, particularly when we start to think about the entire globe and the next generation. You may think this is starting to sound like the beginning of a call to socialist revolution, and that's not off base, since the discipline of sociology has a foundation in Karl Marx. However, the purpose of the sociological imagination isn't to promote the collective over the individual but to help distinguish between them and recognize the intricacies so that we can see the societal issues that affect us and make better personal choices in the context of larger social forces. The variation over time in the Christian understanding of vocation and the idea of nature itself introduced earlier in this chapter show that social context influences human perspective. The sociological imagination provides an opportunity to try to see that influence today, as a member of a specific culture in a specific time and place.

What if we applied a kind of "ecological imagination" in this vein to serving the needs of nature? Just as society emerges from individuals in a network of relationships, so does an ecosystem. Ecosystems include all living and nonliving things in the natural world in relationship with each other. That everything in nature is connected to everything else could be considered a scientific law (i.e., a generalization of the patterns we observe in nature). Humans are a part of the ecosystem because we depend on resources derived from the earth. One perspective on these relationships is the global carbon cycle: carbon dioxide enters the atmosphere, is taken up by plants, consumed by herbivores that eat plants and the carnivores that eat them, and then released back into the atmosphere through respiration when those things eventually die and are decomposed or are burned. Humans are a part of this cycle: we breathe, burn fossil fuels and firewood, die and decompose, and eat plants and animals. Energy for all living things flows through the carbon cycle. This is an oversimplification and generalization of the carbon cycle, but it is one that imagines all living things, and even the atmosphere itself, as potential neighbors. Using a different framework—the water cycle versus the carbon cycle, the ecological niche (i.e., the habitat and role of an organism), or the structure and changes in populations over time—might lead to a different set of neighbors and a different call to action to serve them. Getting to know the natural world rationally, albeit in an imperfect human way, is one way God might call you to serve nature.

Because we often cannot personally observe the direct effects of our actions on ecological neighbors, it takes an element of trust in scientists and our collective understanding of nature to be able to imagine those neighbors. To some extent, even if just by virtue of going to school and learning some of what you were taught, you share in that trust and collective understanding. You can learn about these more distant potential neighbors by becoming educated about nature. This will involve a persistent effort to answer questions such as, What can I observe? What does it do? Where does it go? How does it do that? For most people, this education will primarily consist of reading and listening to scientists and other professionals; others might become the experts and try to answer these questions themselves. Either way, this kind of education is inherently limited because everything you find will be a product of humans, particularly those of your current culture and context, who could very well be wrong.

Reason alone is insufficient to guide you in your vocation of caring for the earth—or any vocation—due to your humanity. In "Reflections of a Young Man on the Choice of a Profession," penned in 1835, Karl Marx described reason as "deceived by emotion and blinded by fantasy." Marx recognized human selfishness at the heart of this issue: "Everyone has a goal which appears to be great, at least to himself, and is great when deepest conviction, the innermost voice of the heart, pronounces it great. . . . We must seriously ask ourselves, therefore, whether we are really inspired about a vocation, whether an inner voice approves of it, or whether the inspiration was a deception, whether that which we took as the Deity's calling to us was self-deceit. But how else could we recognize this except by searching for the source of our inspiration?"[20] As such, a pragmatist could use reason to focus on whatever is most useful for the self, an Epicurean on what's most satisfying for the self, and a utilitarian on what most benefits the majority of humans.

As a complement to reasoning, another way to approach discerning a call to serve is to think about your values. If there's value in nature, it points to a corresponding responsibility to protect it and take care of it, just as someone would take care of a valued possession or person. As you may recall from childhood, not putting away toys can sometimes lead to them being lost or broken. Humans understand ourselves to be a moral species, using what's good, right, and true to determine how we should live. Values are a way of orienting ourselves to make judgments about what "could be" versus "should be." Could I have lower energy use? Should I? Those are two different but related questions, and my answer rests in large part on how I value and view nature. A pragmatist focused on survival, an Epicurean focused on re-creation, or a utilitarian focused on reducing environmental damage might all emphasize the instrumental value of nature (i.e., its value for humans' sake). Alternatively, a wilderness conservationist might emphasize the intrinsic value of nature (i.e., nature's value for its own sake). Both don't seem to align clearly with Christian vocation. The first appears selfish, while the second excludes God's divinity and eliminates the sacred aspect to the role of humans as guardians of the earth. Both also don't seem to align with how humans make decisions, lacking any association with the goal of living a good life.[21]

Thinking instead about relational values that derive from relationships and responsibilities to them might help with discerning vocation. God created and creates nature and thus values all of it, including humans. It is, after all, "very good" in his divine judgment. He put humans into a relationship with the rest of creation as caretakers called to serve (*avad*) and keep (*shamar*) it. What does it look like for all of nature to be very good to God? There are a couple of clues in Scripture: animals (including humans) are fruitful and multiply (see Genesis 1:22), and the land brings forth vegetation (see Genesis 1:11). How are we to understand this from our human perspective? Considering what the very good life looks like for humans and other members of the natural world requires thinking through foundations of well-being and how you value them. For example, if your primary value for nature is instrumental, then you might consider choosing to use less energy as a personal loss, a "less good" life for you. If your primary value for nature is relational, then you might feel called to use less energy, welcoming it (albeit perhaps suffering through it as well) as a way to help nature live a very good life. What does this very good life look like for nature? Is a predator eating prey good and its starvation bad? Is the converse true for the prey? Is a higher population better than a lower one? Are more species better than fewer? Is extinction bad? Much of the difficulty in serving nature is in identifying what's good for a neighbor that doesn't share human morals and living conditions. Reflecting on what you think a very good life looks like for other animals, or an ecosystem, or even the moon might be a way to let the ecological imagination loose as you think through your call to serve nature.

Because we're humans, our values are tied up in our world view just as our reasoning is. Consider Saint Francis of Assisi and his cricket friend, in which a "good life" for nature included a worshipful relationship with the Creator and a brotherhood with humanity. In contrast, Aldo Leopold described a land ethic by saying, "A thing is right when it tends to preserve the integrity, stability, and beauty of the biotic community. It is wrong when it tends otherwise."[22] His idea of the good life for nature reflects his conservationist world view rooted in the idea that nature can take care of itself and is consistent (at least, if not for the interference of those pesky humans). What's considered good and virtuous varies in concert with the other elements of a world view. Intentionally considering the ideas and values you hold about nature, as well as reflecting on those held by your Creator, could open a door to serve nature as your neighbor.

## Cultivating a Relationship with Nature

In Judeo-Christian theology, the cradle of nature and humanity was a garden. If you have ever had a garden, you know that gardens aren't self-sustaining but rather require tending that takes time and effort. Soil must be tilled and prepared, seeds sowed, and plants must be watered, pruned, weeded, protected from critters, nourished . . . , and if all goes well (ask any gardener how often that happens), the resulting crops can be harvested. The next season, the work begins anew. If left to fallow, plants will wither and die, the garden will be overrun with weeds, and the relationship between garden and gardener will cease to exist. Without the resources of the garden, the gardener may not be able to survive. The garden won't flourish without many acts of service from the gardener, nor will the gardener flourish without the garden.

A gardener cultivates a relationship with the plants in the garden by spending time with them, trying to understand their needs, doing things to ease their burdens, giving gifts, and (cue the crazy plant lady) even saying words of appreciation and affection. These investments of time, empathy, energy, resources, and encouragement take effort, effort that can be as unpleasant, monotonous, exhausting, and painful as any other work. Some people with "green thumbs" seem to have an easier go of it, perhaps due to a natural talent. Some regions of the world are more fertile than others, and some plants are less particular about their necessary conditions for growth. It's easy to recognize that keeping a garden is one way to cultivate a relationship with nature and that these plant "neighbors" are served by the gardener's actions. If you have a garden, then—*voilà*—you have a vocation as a gardener, including all the joy and suffering (with the post-Eden weeds) that come along with it.

By analogy, consider all of nature as the garden and you as the gardener. Consider an animal species, the air, or a plant in a pot in your house. Substitute your parents or a friend or any number of others as the garden and you as the gardener. It works for any of those because this isn't a metaphor about caring for a garden specifically but about caring for any other with whom you're in relationship. The golden rule can be applied regardless (see Matthew 7:12). So treat nature just like you would want to be treated, or how you've treated others, and you'll be serving it in vocation.

## Seeds of Hope

As opposed to this idealistic garden metaphor, there's sometimes an overwhelming rhetoric surrounding the environment as a social-ecological issue. We generally hear the story of humans destroying nature. There's evidence that this may be true, but the narrative is perhaps shortsighted or one-sided. It can make it seem hopeless, as if there's no chance of saving the whales, the earth, or anything else. Humanity itself seems imperiled. So why even try?

The Christian narrative of a good creation, disruptive fall, and redemption and restoration provides hope for all of nature. God has used nature to sustain you with your daily bread. God has a plan for all of creation, and humans through vocation can help enact it. You're personally called to do so. Fortunately, you're not called to save the whole world, all the whales, or even one whale. Saving all of nature is Christ's job that will be completed with his second coming (see Revelation 21:1–6). In the meantime, every human is individually called through one's relationship with nature to share in a sacred call to "tend" the earth and, in faith, even to please God by doing so. Martin Luther said this in *The Freedom of a Christian*:

> Adam was created righteous, acceptable, and without sin. He had no need from his labor in the garden to be made righteous and acceptable to God. Rather, the Lord gave Adam work in order to cultivate and protect the garden. This would have been the freest of all works because they were done simply to please God and not to obtain righteousness. . . . The works of the person who trusts God are to be understood in a similar manner. Through faith we are restored to paradise and created anew. We have no need of works in order to be righteous; however, in order to avoid idleness and so that the body might be cared for and disciplined, works are done freely to please God.[23]

God is at work in the cosmos. I urge you to examine your beliefs and values, build a relationship with nature, imagine what could and should be, and heed the call to care for all of creation.

## Exercises for Reflection and Discussion

1. Just as you would sit and have a conversation with a fellow human to get to know them, you can do the same with nature. Go somewhere outside, initially sit still and be quiet, and use your senses to interact with the world around you. Try to sit for five minutes. Listen to layers of sound unfold as the wind moves through the trees, birds call, insects hum, and you and other humans (and their human creations) go about your activities. Then see, touch, and smell the things around you, taking time to interact with them intentionally. Just like when interacting with a human, it might be hard to "listen" at first. For one of your nonhuman neighbors, name it, record the details of your observations, and explain how it relates to you and your life.

2. Environmental advocate Barry Commoner, a founder of modern environmentalism, proposed four informal scientific laws of ecology:
   a. Everything is connected to everything else.
   b. Everything must go somewhere.
   c. Nature knows best.
   d. There is no such thing as a free lunch.

   How do these laws reflect a modern world view on nature? If these are accurate reflections of reality, what duties do humans have to nature?

3. There's sociopolitical tension around the responsibility of humans toward nature (see the conversation about climate change as a current example). Do you think conceptualizing this issue as a *sacred* vocation of caring for nature could be a disruptive force? What would be the benefits and shortcomings of such an approach in society?

## Notes

1 Gordon J. Wenham, *Genesis 1–15* (Waco, TX: Word Books, 1987), 33, 38–39.
2 Wenham, 67.
3 William C. Placher, *Callings: Twenty Centuries of Christian Wisdom on Vocation* (Grand Rapids: Eerdmans, 2005), 5–9.
4 Annie Dillard, *Pilgrim at Tinker Creek* (New York: Harper, 1974), 33.
5 Paul J. Crutzen, "The 'Anthropocene,'" in *Earth System Science in the Anthropocene*, ed. Eckart Ehlers and Thomas Krafft (Berlin: Springer, 2006), 13–18.
6 Peter Singer, *Animal Liberation: A New Ethics for Our Treatment of Animals* (New York: HarperCollins, 1975), 205.
7 Aldo Leopold, *A Sand County Almanac: With Essays on Conservation from Round River* (New York: Ballantine, 1970), 264.
8 William Cronon, "The Trouble with Wilderness: Or, Getting Back to the Wrong Nature," *Environmental History* 1, no. 1 (1996): 7–28.
9 See chapter 3 of Darwin's *On the Origin of Species*, first published in 1859.
10 Henry David Thoreau, "Walking," *Atlantic*, June 1862, accessed January 6, 2020, https://www.theatlantic.com/magazine/archive/1862/06/walking/304674/.

11  Henry David Thoreau, *The Writings of Henry David Thoreau: Journal, March 2, 1859–November 30, 1859*, ed. Bradford Torrey (Boston: Houghton Mifflin, 1906), 387.

12  Wilderness Act of 1964, Pub. L. No. 88-577 (16 U.S.C. 1131-1136), Section 2C, accessed January 6, 2020, https://winapps.umt.edu/winapps/media2/wilderness/NWPS/documents/publiclaws/PDF/The_Wilderness_Act.pdf.

13  United Nations Environmental Programme—World Conservation Monitoring Centre, *Protected Area Profile for United States of America from the World Database of Protected Areas, January 2020*, accessed on January 10, 2020, https://www.protectedplanet.net/country/US.

14  US Department of Commerce: Economics and Statistics Administration, Census Bureau, *1990 Census of Population and Housing: Population and Housing Units* (Washington, DC: US Government Printing Office, 1990), table 4, accessed January 6, 2020, https://www.census.gov/prod/cen1990/cph2/cph-2-1-1.pdf.

15  Oliver R. W. Pergrams and Patricia A. Zaradic, "Evidence for a Fundamental and Pervasive Shift away from Nature-Based Recreation," *Proceedings of the National Academy of Sciences of the United States of America* 105, no. 7 (2008): 2295–2300.

16  Selin Kesebir and Pelin Kesebir, "A Growing Disconnection from Nature Is Evident in Cultural Products," *Perspectives on Psychological Science* 12, no. 2 (2017): 258–69.

17  Andrew Balmford, Lizzie Clegg, Tim Coulson, and Jennie Taylor, "Why Conservationists Should Heed Pokémon," *Science*, March 29, 2002, 2367.

18  Richard Louv, *Last Child in the Woods: Saving Our Children from Nature-Deficit Disorder* (Chapel Hill, NC: Algonquin, 2008), 2.

19  The previous quote comes from page 44 of London's *The Call of the Wild* (New York: Dover, 1990).

20  Karl Marx, *Writings of the Yong Marx on Philosophy and Society*, trans. L. David Easton and Kurt H. Guddat (Garden City, NY: Doubleday, 1967), 36.

21  Kai M. A. Chan et al., "Opinion: Why Protect Nature? Rethinking Values and the Environment," *Proceedings of the National Academy of Sciences* 113, no. 6 (2016): 1462–65.

22  Leopold, *Sand County Almanac*, 262.

23  Martin Luther, *The Freedom of a Christian* (1520), trans. Mark D. Tranvik (Minneapolis: Fortress, 2008), 73–74.

# Knit Together in Love

## Vocation in Marriage and Family Life

*Buddy Mendez*

## Marriage and Family Life Is a Gift from God

The fundamental teaching about Christian vocation in marriage and family life is that our calling into marriage and family life is both a divine calling and a gift from God. "God settles the solitary in a home," proclaims Psalm 68:6. God also provides the direction we ought to pursue in marriage and family life for the mutual benefit of all family members. Because God created humans to crave relational connection, he calls husbands and wives to find ultimate intimacy and oneness in marriage (see Genesis 2:18). The gift of marriage allows spouses to fulfill their divine calling to "be fruitful and multiply" (Genesis 1:28), creating a safe and secure foundation (family life) from which children can move into and live in alignment with their divine design and purpose (see Proverbs 22:6).

The purpose of this chapter is to provide practical biblical and psychological guidance on how best to use your God-given vocations in marriage and family life to love and to care for others as husband and wife, mother and father, son and daughter, and brother and sister. This chapter also offers guidance on temporary callings that people often have before marriage: boyfriend and girlfriend.

## Our Calling in Marriage: What the Bible Says to Husbands and Wives

The bedrock of any family is marriage. The strength of any marriage positively correlates with the well-being of the entire family system. In my early days as a psychotherapist, I worked for two years at a psychiatric hospital for adolescents. During my stay, I never found a troubled teen who didn't come from a distressed marriage. It was truly remarkable and a valuable lesson that prompted my subsequent focus in my private practice in marital therapy.

My focus on marriage as a Christian psychotherapist has led me to discover what the Bible says about marriage. The first biblical truth I noticed is that men and women are different. Genesis 1:27 reads, "So God created man in his own image, in the image of God he created him; male and female he created them." If males and females are different, then it logically follows that husbands and wives have different needs. Indeed, my own experience as a Clinical psychologist has confirmed this notion. In my work with hundreds of couples over the past twenty-five years, I've seen the following trends. Wives tend to want to feel secure, cherished, esteemed, pursued, and emotionally intimate with their husbands. On the other hand, husbands tend to want to feel significant, affirmed, and respected.

Taking this line of thinking a step further, if husbands and wives have different needs, it makes perfect sense why God has called husbands and wives to different roles in marriage. Thus the purpose of assigning different roles in Christian marriage isn't to diminish the value or status of men and women but to effectively satisfy their different needs. Remember, we all have equal status in the eyes of God because we're all made "in the image of God." The apostle Paul affirmed this truth of our equal standing when he wrote in his letter to the Galatians, "There is neither Jew nor Greek, there is neither slave nor free, there is no male and female, for you are all one in Christ Jesus" (Galatians 3:28). The purpose of our God-given role assignments is to enable spouses to love each other in ways that feel loving. What are the biblically assigned roles of husbands and wives? In Ephesians 5:21–33, Paul answers this important question. Verse 25 reads, "Husbands, love your wives, as Christ loved the church and gave himself up for her." Next is a list of practical ways husbands can love their wives as Christ loved the church by living and dying for it:

- Talk to her to connect and not to solve problems.
- Express affection often and without sexual intention.
- Share your heart, challenges, and victories with her.
- Speak to her gently, without sarcasm and teasing.
- Say to her, "I'm sorry."
- Stay patiently engaged in conflict rather than quickly yielding or retreating.
- Never threaten divorce.
- Treasure and cherish her.
- Value her perspectives (see Proverbs 31:26).
- Praise her in front of the children, family, and friends (see Proverbs 31:28).
- Allow her to help you (see Genesis 2:18).

Wives are encouraged to "submit" (verse 22) and "respect" their husbands (verse 33). Submitting doesn't mean blind obedience to ungodly demands. Rather, it means avoiding the temptation to quarrel and resist a husband's attempt to lead as Christ leads the church through humble service and sacrificial love. Some practical ways of showing submission and respect include the following:

- Allow your husband to lead as Christ leads.
- Trust that your husband has your best interests in his heart.
- Affirm your husband rather than shame him (see Proverbs 12:4).
- Be pleasant with your words (see Proverbs 16:24).
- Compliment him when he serves you or the children.
- Say to him, "I believe in you."
- Tell him how content you are with your life together.
- Praise his desire to protect and to provide for the family.
- Honor him in front of the children and differ with him in private.
- Ask him for his ideas and opinions.
- Enjoy sexual connection with him (see Proverbs 5:18–19).

Finally, it's important to note that Ephesians 5:21 advocates "submitting to one another out of reverence for Christ." This means that husbands and wives should serve each other not because of the worthiness of each other but because of how Christ first loved each of them (see 1 John 4:7–11). In other words, we're encouraged to serve our spouse even when we believe our spouse isn't holding up his or her end of the bargain. A former professor of mine at Fuller Seminary, John Finch, put it this way: "Do your duty with faith in God without attachment to the fruit of the action." The benefit of this approach from a psychological perspective is that when one spouse unilaterally fulfills his or her God-prescribed role, the other spouse will respond in kind and the couple will move into a mutually reinforcing positive feedback loop of loving actions.

The Bible offers additional insight and guidance on marriage in the often-quoted passage from Genesis 2:24 (KJV), "Therefore shall a man *leave* his father and his mother, and shall *cleave* unto his wife: and they shall *be one flesh*" (emphasis mine). The following is a discussion of what this means practically.

### Leaving (Maturity)

Maturity in marriage refers to the psychological and spiritual development of each spouse. It reflects the extent to which spouses are able to act with an age-appropriate degree of autonomy while also accepting responsibility for their decisions and behaviors. Psychological research has shown that maturity is highly associated with overall marital adjustment.[1] Furthermore, emotional maturity positively correlates with marital satisfaction.

Spiritual maturity and psychological maturity are reciprocally related. One can't exist without the other, and each enhances the growth of the other. Together they promote a strong and healthy marital bond. There are three important components to maturity: putting away childish behaviors, giving up old habits, and developing growth-promoting character traits.

First, each spouse needs to *put away childish behaviors.* Paul puts it this way when talking about Christian maturity in general: "When I was a child, I spoke like a child, I thought like a child, I

reasoned like a child. When I became a man, I gave up childish ways"
(1 Corinthians 13:11). Next is a list of childish behaviors that can lead
to trouble in marriage:

- selfishness
- pouting
- demanding one's way
- seeking immediate gratification
- low frustration tolerance
- emotional reasoning
- making excuses and blaming others
- inflexibility
- dishonesty
- conditional love
- avoiding confrontation and conflict

The second component of maturity is *giving up habitual ways*
of relating to one's husband or wife that were adaptive in the past but
are maladaptive in the present. Doing this can be difficult because
there's often a false belief deep in one's heart that the best approach
to future relationships is to do what's worked in the past. Because
of this, anxiety arises when a different approach is considered. In
order to reduce this anticipatory anxiety, a spouse resorts to the old
methods even when they're consistently ineffective.

Consider the hypothetical case of Tim. Tim grew up in a family where verbal expressions of affirmation were discouraged in
order to promote the core family virtue of humility. Now Tim is
married to Lily, and one of Lily's main complaints is that Tim is too
stingy with words of affirmation and can't respond to a compliment
without being self-dismissive. In this case, Tim's approach to verbal affirmation worked very well in his family of origin; however, it
doesn't work well with his wife. This is likely because Lily's family of
origin promoted verbal praise and viewed such praise as an expression of love. On the other hand, Tim has inferred from his own
family of origin experiences that verbal affirmations promote pride
and aren't a means of expressing love. The problem is that if Tim is
going to love Lily in a way that feels loving to her, he's going to have

to act in a counterintuitive way. He'll have to give up the old pattern of withholding positive affirmations.

Next is a list of behaviors that are often helpful in a person's family of origin but detrimental in one's current marriage. Maybe you've witnessed these behaviors in marriages before:

- compulsively performing in order to be valued
- interrupting and loud talking in order to be recognized
- downplaying one's own successes to make others feel better
- giving the silent treatment to communicate hurt and anger
- acting strong even when feeling weak to avoid being shamed
- suppressing feelings to avoid feeling dismissed
- avoiding conflict to maintain peace
- not relying on others to avoid feeling like a burden
- yielding to the wishes of others to avoid tension

The third component of maturity is *developing growth-promoting character traits*. An exhaustive listing of such traits could be the topic of an entire book. For our purposes, I've identified six growth-promoting traits found in the Bible: perseverance, accepting feedback, initiative, self-control, standing firm, and self-awareness.

*Perseverance*: James connects perseverance and maturity in the Christian life when he writes, "And let steadfastness have its full effect, that you may be perfect [or, mature] and complete, lacking in nothing" (James 1:4). Spouses who persevere continue to love even when they receive nothing in return. They don't despair in adverse circumstances or undesirable outcomes. They know what God wants them to do, and they do it out of love for God, not in order to attain some positive outcome. They have faith that ultimately things will work together for good even when in the midst of current trials and tribulations (see Romans 8:28).

Another aspect of perseverance involves refusing to quit. I've observed in my private practice that the most meaningful actions are often the hardest to do. However, they aren't impossible. With practice and repetition, behaviors that at one time seemed difficult can become a regular part of one's life.

*Accepting feedback*: In Proverbs 27:17, we read, "Iron sharpens iron, and one man sharpens another." In marriage, husbands and wives have the potential to either sharpen or alienate each other with feedback. It all depends on how the feedback is both given and received. It's best to give feedback in a calm and kind tone of voice and to stick to the facts. When receiving feedback, it's best to ask, Is there some truth to what my spouse is saying? Remember, God can speak truth through an imperfect human being. Therefore, it's important not to fall into a defensive posture such as counterattacking, making excuses, or blaming others.

*Initiative*: This refers to proactive behavior that addresses the needs of one's spouse. Simply stated, it's doing what needs to be done without having to be asked. Spouses who take the initiative work hard to create a climate conducive to positive behavioral change in their spouse rather than feeling helpless and hopeless when desired changes aren't occurring.

Consider the hypothetical case of Jack. Jack feels discouraged because his wife, Carla, continues to say she's too tired for intimacy at the end of the day. Instead of lamenting his poor choice of a sexual partner, Jack can create an environment that contributes to Carla being less tired and more sexually interested. This can include a variety of things such as helping out more with the children and the household chores, taking Carla out on romantic dates, complementing Carla on her appearance, and possibly even hiring a housekeeper.

*Self-control*: People often believe that it's healthy to suppress emotions. I disagree. Emotions aren't the problem. The problem is how we respond to emotions, especially intense emotions. The issue for couples is how to respond in healthy ways when anger, frustration, pain, and fear are flooding their hearts. The Bible warns us that "a man without self-control is like a city broken into and left without walls" (Proverbs 25:28). Paul gives Christians this guidance about their emotions and responses: "Be angry and do not sin" (Ephesians 4:26). Husbands and wives with self-control don't respond automatically and impulsively. Rather, they stop, pay attention to their feelings, think about a proper response, and then execute that response. Self-control is like a muscle. If you exercise it, then it will grow stronger.

*Standing firm*: This refers to the act of holding fast to a conviction despite resistance from one's spouse. Consider the hypothetical case of Spencer and Joan. Spencer explains to his wife, Joan, that they can save money on taxes by not claiming the cash money he earned in his construction business this year. Joan believes this is unethical and goes against the command of Jesus to "render to Caesar the things that are Caesar's" (Matthew 22:21). Spencer teases Joan saying that she knows nothing about the realities of the business world and should stop sticking her nose in his business. He adds that they can use the extra money for the children's educational expenses. In this example, Joan would do well to hold her ground that they abide by the law. This choice aligns her with Paul who encouraged fellow Christians to "stand firm" in the faith (see 1 Corinthians 16:13; Galatians 5:1; Ephesians 6:14; and Colossians 4:12).

*Self-awareness*: There are several ways spouses can develop an increased understanding of why they do what they do. People can learn about themselves through self-observation, introspection, listening to God (see Psalm 139:1–4 and Romans 7:7), and feedback from others. One of the best ways to develop self-awareness is through professional counseling. Many people are averse to this option because they assume that only "crazy" people are in psychotherapy. I wholeheartedly disagree. Psychotherapy with a competent counselor can be one of the richest and most rewarding experiences for anyone interested in growth and development. A wise counselor can help us understand the conscious and unconscious reasons behind our thoughts, feelings, and behavior (see Proverbs 20:5). In terms of marriage, a well-trained counselor can teach spouses how to relate to each other in more loving, productive, and healthy ways.

## Cleaving (Commitment)

Genesis 2:24 (KJV) says that after leaving his parents, a man "shall cleave unto his wife" in marriage. The Bible's simple teaching on this commitment is "once married, always married." Jesus put it this way: "What therefore God has joined together, let not man separate" (Matthew 19:6). This perspective is quite different from the secular view of marriage that says, "I will stay married to you as long as I feel I am in love with you." The problem with the secular view is that it's perfectly normal for feelings of love to wax and wane. For engaged and newly married couples, this may be hard to believe. However, any couple who's been married for longer than five years will tell you that romantic and passionate feelings come and go throughout the course of even healthy marriages.

Therefore, the decision to stay or leave one's marriage should never be contingent on feelings. Instead, Christians should choose to love each other in the same unconditional manner that Christ has chosen to love us. The Bible confirms the truth that love is action-oriented in this famous passage in 1 Corinthians 13:4–7: "Love is patient and kind; love does not envy or boast; it is not arrogant or rude. It does not insist on its own way; it is not irritable or resentful; it does not rejoice at wrongdoing, but rejoices with the truth. Love bears all things, believes all things, hopes all things, endures all things." Although feelings of love are enjoyable and desirable, they aren't a necessary condition for love to exist. When feelings of love fade, couples need not panic. Rather, they should see these times as opportunities to extend love through actions until loving feelings inevitably return. This can only be done as couples make a commitment to love one another in spite of how they may feel at any particular moment and regardless of how their spouses respond to their gestures of love.

Contemporary research findings support the notion that couples who stay committed through the tough times can regain the happiness they once had. In a longitudinal study reported by the Institute for American Values, researchers found that of 645 unhappy spouses, 2 out of 3 who chose not to divorce or separate ended up happily married five years later.[2]

From a Christian perspective, three types of commitment strengthen marriages. They are commitment to God, commitment to one's spouse, and commitment to the welfare of the marriage. The first and most important commitment is to God (see Matthew 22:36–37). Paul, in Romans 12:1–2, explains the commitment this way: "I appeal to you therefore, brothers, by the mercies of God, to present your bodies as a living sacrifice, holy and acceptable to God, which is your spiritual worship. Do not be conformed to this world, but be transformed by the renewal of your mind, that by testing you may discern what is the will of God, what is good and acceptable and perfect." In other words, we're to worship God with our whole lives.

The second commitment is to one's spouse. Paul, in Ephesians 5:21–27, provides the following guidance:

> [Submit] to one another out of reverence for Christ. Wives, submit to your own husbands, as to the Lord. For the husband is the head of the wife even as Christ is the head of the church, his body, and is himself its Savior. Now as the church submits to Christ, so also wives should submit in everything to their husbands. Husbands, love your wives, as Christ loved the church and gave himself up for her, that he might sanctify her, having cleansed her by the washing of water with the word, so that he might present the church to himself in splendor, without spot or wrinkle or any such thing, that she might be holy and without blemish.

This commitment to sacrificial service includes husbands "cleansing" and "washing" their wives, which happens in forgiveness. To forgive doesn't mean excusing, ignoring, or tolerating painful feelings and sinful actions. It means that husbands resist the urge to retaliate in response to being hurt by hurting back. Our ability to forgive is never perfect because of our sinful nature. However, if spouses make every effort to forgive one another, marital commitment will strengthen and marital satisfaction will rise.

Our third commitment is to the marriage. This type of commitment is described as "personal dedication" by Scott Stanley, Daniel Trathen, Savanna McCain, and Milt Bryan in their book, *A Lasting Promise*.[3] According to these researchers, personal dedication comprises the following five characteristics.

*The priority of the relationship*: The relationship takes priority over work, children, parents, money, and even ministry. One of the things I'm constantly battling in my work with couples is their tendency to attend to other matters of life before they attend to their marriage. The most common dynamics I see are husbands prioritizing work over marriage and wives prioritizing children over husbands. Often couples are just too tired to interact with each other in any meaningful way because they've expended energy attending to less important matters throughout the day. By the time these couples are ready to focus on each other, all they can think about is sleep.

*Alternative monitoring*: This pertains to our ability to resist serious consideration of alternative partners. This may involve excessive flirting, indulging in mental fantasies with other people, or even pushing the limits of a platonic friendship. Jesus warns us to resist these temptations when he says, "You have heard that it was said, 'You shall not commit adultery.' But I say to you that everyone who looks at a woman with lustful intent has already committed adultery with her in his heart" (Matthew 5:27–28). There's nothing more damaging to a relationship than infidelity, regardless of whether it exists in our behavior or in our hearts. I've seen too many marriages devastated by the consequences of infidelity. The rupture of trust in these cases is a deep and, in some cases, fatal wound to the marriage.

*"We-ness"*: This refers to the degree to which each spouse views his or her relationship as two individuals working together as one team. In my private practice, I often ask couples to come to a "we" decision rather than settle for a "you" or an "I" decision. This helps them resolve conflicts and solve problems. It also leads to a sense of equal participation and fairness in the relationship. Arriving at a "we" decision or solution requires relinquishing one's personal freedom. Spouses can no longer choose to live on their own terms. I often gently remind couples that the decision to marry is a decision to give up a degree of personal autonomy. However, couples working together realize there's a double benefit: what's good for the team is ultimately best for them as individuals. I also remind them that the joys of "oneness" far outweigh the costs.

*Satisfaction with sacrifice*: This refers to our willingness to expend personal resources (such as time, energy, and effort) for our spouse's benefit and the satisfaction we can feel from making those sacrifices. I often share with couples that marriages are like fruit trees. They need to be nourished and cared for in order to mature and to produce good fruit. If a fruit tree is left alone, it will slowly whither, produce less fruit each successive season, and eventually die. Couples need to make the sacrifices that are necessary to give their marriage the water, sunlight, warmth, and rich soil it needs to produce a bountiful harvest for both of them.

*Desiring the long-term:* This refers to a couple's wish for the relationship to work out over the long term. When Christian couples encounter problems, they don't contemplate leaving but focus on finding solutions and making necessary behavioral changes. Spouses who refuse to leave when the going gets tough grow in character.

### Becoming One Flesh (Intimacy)

The biblical phrase "they shall be one flesh" (Genesis 2:24 KJV) beautifully describes the intimacy found in healthy marriages. It implies a comprehensive and seamless union between husband and wife. A bond characterized by psychological, relational, physical, and spiritual intimacy.

*Psychological intimacy (self-disclosure):* This refers to an open and honest expression of one's thoughts, feelings, beliefs, values, and attitudes. It is an excellent way to increase intimacy in marriage. Paul writes in his letter to fellow believers in Thessalonica, "So, being affectionately desirous of you, we were ready to share with you not only the gospel of God but also our own selves, because you had become very dear to us" (1 Thessalonians 2:8). This disposition toward openness with the Thessalonians is a helpful example of how to build intimacy in marriage. When we're transparent with our spouse, we allow our relationship to move to a deeper level. In fact, researchers have found that greater depth of self-disclosure correlates with increased intimacy.[4]

Husbands and wives often feel conflicted when it comes to self-disclosure. A part of us wants to "know" and to "be known." This makes perfect sense, since God created us to be relationally connected. The Bible tells us that even before sin entered the world, it was not good for man to be alone (see Genesis 2:18). However, because of sin in the world, another part of us fears that open disclosure can be dangerous. We worry that our spouse may respond negatively when we psychologically reveal our deepest parts in his or her presence. We fear our spouse's disappointment, rejection, and in some cases, even abandonment.

In order to protect ourselves from the potential undesirable consequences of self-disclosure, we often hide our true selves. We hide in a variety of ways, such as staying busy, staying quiet, changing the subject, speaking generally, keeping conversations superficial, gossiping about others, focusing on the children, watching television, surfing the internet, and giving vague or short answers to questions.

The problem with hiding is that it ultimately deprives us of the intimacy we crave. Hiding can only protect us from pain by cutting off our access to intimacy. Self-disclosure is the road to psychological intimacy, and when we choose to avoid this road, we can't reach our desired destination. If we continually avoid self-disclosure, our marriage will eventually die a quiet death. Thus we really have no choice. We must push past our fears. Despite the very real risks, we must find the courage to share our innermost thoughts and feelings with our spouse.

Such boldness is only possible when we rely on God to meet our needs for safety, security, and significance. We need to remind ourselves what God has done and continues to do for us. When we feel anxious, God gives us peace. When we feel guilty, he forgives us. When we feel ashamed and inferior, he reminds us of our value and worth. When we feel alone, he comforts us with his loving presence.

*Relational intimacy*: This refers to the degree to which husbands and wives feel emotionally connected. There's a sense of closeness and comfortableness when talking, playing, or just hanging out together. Spouses who are relationally intimate rely on each other in times of need. They speak to each other frequently and trust that disclosures are confidential. They function as a team and have a strong camaraderie, fondness, and admiration for each other. They also have common interests and enjoy each other's company. They laugh, play, cry, and dream together. They consider their beloved spouse to be their best friend (see Song of Solomon 5:16).

*Physical intimacy*: It may come as a surprise to some that the oneness mandated by God for marriage includes physical intimacy. Research has found that physical intimacy actually promotes and maintains attachment in marriage.[5] Powerful hormones (oxytocin for women and vasopressin for men) are released by the brain during sexual intercourse that promote bonding, thus helping couples comply with the biblical mandate not to break up what God has joined together. It's vital, therefore, to keep the fire of passion alive and well throughout marriage.

Another common surprise is that Scripture has a high view of sexual passion in marriage. Song of Solomon speaks frequently and positively about the wonders and joys of sex. Here's an excerpt from this eloquent and poetic tribute to passion and desire:

[He]
How beautiful are your feet in sandals, O noble daughter!
Your rounded thighs are like jewels, the work of a master hand.
Your navel is a rounded bowl that never lacks mixed wine.
Your belly is a heap of wheat, encircled with lilies.
Your two breasts are like two fawns, twins of a gazelle. (Song of Solomon 7:1–3)


[He]
I say I will climb the palm tree and lay hold of its fruit.
Oh may your breasts be like clusters of the vine,
and the scent of your breath like apples,
and your mouth like the best wine.


[She]
It goes down smoothly for my beloved, gliding over lips and teeth.
I am my beloved's, and his desire is for me. (Song of Solomon 7:8–10)

Sexual passion is a God-given joy. It's also each spouse's responsibility to satisfy each other's sexual needs and thereby avoid being tempted into sexual immorality (see 1 Corinthians 7:2–4).

In my private practice, husbands and wives often complain that don't have enough intimacy. The problem is that they're talking about two different things. Men are saying, "I want more sexual intercourse." Women are saying, "I want more conversation, romance, affection, and foreplay." Husbands who pay attention to these broader aspects of physical intimacy are more likely to satisfy their wives and have more satisfying sex lives.

*Spiritual intimacy*: This is probably the most crucial area of intimacy for a Christian couple. Examples of spiritual intimacy include spouses studying the Bible, attending church, praying, listening to sacred music, and talking about their personal spiritual journeys together. You've probably heard the saying that "the couple that prays together stays together." Research by Roman Catholic priest and sociologist Andrew Greeley has found incredible support for this notion. In his analysis of 657 couples throughout the US, Greeley found that 90 percent of couples who prayed together and were sexually satisfied reported feeling very happy in their marriage. Furthermore, 60 percent of couples who weren't sexually satisfied but still prayed together reported feeling very happy with their marriage.[6]

Prayer has several benefits for couples. Most importantly, prayer is a powerful means by which we invite God to participate in our marriage. The acknowledgment of God's presence and control can lead to an increased sense of security that allows us to relate to each other with authenticity, honesty, and vulnerability. When we pray to God, who knows everything, there's no need to hide or to put up a front. It's healthy for our spouse to hear us relate to God in such a vulnerable, humble, and dependent manner. This helps us grow in empathy and understanding for one another and leads to greater feelings of closeness and compassion.

## Dating: Whom and How?

Young people often seek and get to know possible marriage partners by dating first as boyfriend and girlfriend. While these callings are temporary, it's still worth considering whom and how to date so that the dating relationship goes well and positively impacts a potential marriage.

Selection is extremely important in the dating process. If you don't select well, the struggles encountered in dating can quickly become insurmountable. Next are some guidelines for choosing a dating partner.

*Date someone with good character*: Dating relationships have a high potential for risk and reward. It's wise to scan for "red flags" and to end the relationship when the risks become too great. Some bad character traits to watch out for are dishonesty, failure to keep commitments, manipulation, coercion, inappropriate aggression, detachment, possessiveness, competitiveness, distrust, dismissiveness, irresponsibility, lack of self-control, contempt, and defensiveness.

When you find a dating partner with good character traits, the dating relationship will likely flourish. Look for someone who's compassionate, humble, and patient (see Colossians 3:12).

*Date someone wise*: Ask yourself if the person you're interested in dating makes wise choices in life. A person who makes wise decisions will likely help you live wisely and honorably too (see Proverbs 13:20).

*Date someone like-minded*: Psychologists have found that marriages are more likely to thrive when couples have shared religious values at the outset.[7] Since people often date as a means of discerning who might be a suitable spouse, it logically follows that it's wise to date someone who shares your core beliefs and can be your spiritual partner (see Deuteronomy 7:1–3 and 2 Corinthians 6:14).

*Listen to your parents*: Even though it might be hard for young people to accept, parents can identify their children's blind spots in selecting a dating partner. Parents typically know their children well and have experienced life in greater breadth and depth. When you value your parents' advice, you honor them and protect yourself from unforeseen harm (see Exodus 20:12).

Because dating involves a high degree of vulnerability, it's important to respect your dating partner. Disrespectful actions in dating often lead to painful feelings of anxiety, depression, and isolation. Next are a few guidelines on how to date others with respect.

*Help with growth*: In dating, it's tempting to expend vast amounts of time and energy on your personal gratification rather than on your partner's growth. In a respectful dating relationship, though, your fulfillment is secondary to your partner's personal development. For instance, dating couples might not offer each other helpful feedback to preserve peace in the relationship. However, constructive confrontation, even if personally uncomfortable, can promote growth in each other (see Proverbs 27:17).

*Act with love*: Love is much more than a romantic feeling. This emotion comes and goes. Lasting love cares for others with patience and humility (see 1 Corinthians 13:4–7). Pursuing this love brings joy and growth to the dating relationship and honors the love God has first shown us in Christ.

*Treat with purity*: Physical attraction is very powerful, pulling dating partners toward sexual intimacy. It's for this reason that

Scripture directs us "not stir up or awaken love until it pleases" (Song of Solomon 2:7). In other words, wait until marriage to have sexual relations. This preserves your sexual virtue and the purity of the person you're dating (see 1 Thessalonians 4:3–7). It also keeps the bearing and raising of children within marriage. Remember, with every temptation to sin, God provides an alternative to sin (see 1 Corinthians 10:13). This gives hope to those who wrestle with sexual temptation in a dating relationship.

## Our Calling as Parents

Sexual intimacy in marriage naturally leads husbands and wives toward fulfilling God's call for them to "be fruitful and multiply" (Genesis 1:28 NSV). Bearing children brings spouses another divine calling: being parents. Our calling as parents includes participating in three distinct roles: counselor, comforter, and authority.

### Parent as Counselor

Parents do well to take on the role of counselor when they see their child struggling in life. In this role, parents explore and understand their child's internal world of thoughts, feelings, and meanings. A helpful acrostic for doing this is LOVE.

L stands for "Listen Carefully." Listening before speaking is both practically wise and biblically encouraged (see James 1:19). Parents should first hear out the entire story that contextualizes what's bothering their child and then ask questions starting with who, what, where, when, why, and how. By listening fully, parents can avoid the trap of making false assumptions and jumping too quickly to giving advice rather than showing support and understanding.

O stands for "Open up Your Child." Parents can facilitate this process by indicating interest and summarizing what they hear their child saying in a concise, coherent, and organized manner.

V stands for "Validate." Validation communicates to one's child that what he feels and thinks matters and is worth understanding. The following phrases are helpful in this regard: "That makes sense to me," "I can understand how you feel that way," and "I understand."

*E* stands for "Empathize." This means that parents demonstrate in words that they can feel the internal experience of their child. In other words, say what you see. Examples of empathic statements are as follows: "That looks scary to you" or "It seems like you aren't sure whether you want to play baseball this season because it takes so much time away from your friends and your other interests."

In addition to exploring their child's internal world, parents act as counselors when they teach and guide their children. Proverbs 22:6 says, "Train up a child in the way he should go; even when he is old he will not depart from it." Deuteronomy 6:6–7 says, "And these words that I command you today shall be on your heart. You shall teach them diligently to your children, and shall talk of them when you sit in your house, and when you walk by the way, and when you lie down, and when you rise." These passages refer to parents teaching their children the knowledge of God and God's ways for life. However, parents also do well to teach and guide their children in all aspects of living life well.

In providing guidance, it's important to avoid the two extremes of overgratification by doing too much for your children and under-gratification by doing too little. For example, if your child asks you to show him how to ask his coach for feedback on why he isn't playing more in the games, you can teach him assertive and respectful communication techniques. However, if your child has already learned how to be assertive and she asks you to talk to the coach for her to avoid feeling embarrassed and anxious, you help her best by politely saying no.

## Parent as Comforter

Parents as comforters soothe and calm their children during times of distress and discouragement. As God (our Father) comforts us (His children) in our afflictions, so we're empowered to comfort our children as they face various afflictions in life (see 2 Corinthians 1:3–4). The Bible refers to several ways brothers and sisters in the faith care for each other, including encouragement, affection, confession and prayer, forgiveness, and unconditional love (see Hebrews 10:24–25; Romans 12:10; James 5:16; Colossians 3:13; and 1 Peter 4:8). These caring ways also apply to how parents can comfort their children.

From a psychological perspective, other helpful ways of comforting children include play, minimizing pressure, and creating positive memories.

*Play*: One of the best and often overlooked ways of comforting children is through play. I often tell my students that a child's favorite toy is his or her parents. Children benefit from play that's unstructured, nondirective, and age-appropriate. Unstructured play allows children to experience freedom and agency in the context of relational connection. Nondirective play facilitates the development of initiative and confidence and reduces anxiety. Age-appropriate play facilitates growth and maturity. In play, children receive their parents' undivided attention and affection without feeling an obligation to perform or please. Play serves as a welcome break from the daily demands of life placed on children by their parents, teachers, coaches, and other adult caretakers.

*Minimizing pressure to perform*: One of the most common complaints I hear from my adolescent clients is that they feel overwhelmed by the stress of constantly striving to perform in school and extracurricular activities at an elite level. These demands are sometimes placed on them by anxious or status-driven parents but oftentimes are self-imposed by the anxious child. Regardless of the origin of the stress, parents who value and emphasize balance between achievement, rest, recreation, and relational connection can help reduce this dangerous pressure to perform and thereby minimize a multitude of negative outcomes such as anxiety, depression, and burn out.

*Creating positive memories*: Positive memories of enjoyable family time inevitably lead to retrieving and reexperiencing that warmth, connection, and contentment. Consider one such memory penned by my eighteen-year-old daughter, Malia:

> There honestly wasn't a ton that all six of us liked; with most things, there was at least one dissenter. However, there was a place that never failed us—the "top of the hill" pool. I didn't realize until high school that this name was our own colloquialism and that this amazing oasis wasn't built for only our family. The last shower to the right was mine, the button for the hot tub jets was my brother's, and the third to last umbrella belonged to my mother. Dad used to put me on his back and

pretend to be a Hawaiian sea turtle. Boys played sharks in the deep end as the girls played mermaids trying to escape their terrifying bite. I remember whipping my hair in circles and vowing that one day it would grow long enough to look like Aquamarine's from my favorite mermaid movie. We loved that pool like another family member, so much so that it dampened our spirits when it had to close for routine maintenance and we had to descend to one of the "lower" pools. I fondly recall how we loved and enjoyed each other's company as we devoured home-packed PB&J's and organic chips and salsa, listened to summer music, played without a care in the world, and generously shared each other's towels when it was time to dry off and head home. The water connected us somehow, and I still feel that interwoven tingling sensation whenever we return to what has become a familiar touchpoint and a life-long friend to our entire family.

## Parent as Authority

In the role of authority figure, parents are careful to discipline their children because they love them (see Proverbs 13:24). The Bible teaches that discipline is helpful to families. Discipline leads to peace and delight for parents (see Proverbs 29:17). In Hebrews 12:7–11, we read that God's discipline leads to righteousness and holiness of life. Thus it seems that if parents discipline in a manner consistent with God's discipline, their children will be encouraged to live a more virtuous life to their benefit and that of others.

In my private practice as a clinical psychologist, I teach parents four elements of effective discipline: clear rules, specific requests, effective follow-through, and consistency.

*Clear rules*: Make a list of rules that corresponds to your core family virtues. Be specific and modify as necessary depending on the life stage of the family and the developmental phase of the children. Examples of clear rules are the following: "Always say please and thank you," "Put everything away where it belongs," "Never antagonize your brother or sister," "Always do what you're told," "Speak respectfully without back talking or whining," "Do your chores on time without having to be asked," and "Always complete your homework before you engage in free-time activities."

*Specific requests*: Whenever your child needs to comply with your request, phrase it in the form of a command and include a time element word. For example, instead of saying, "Can you please load the dishwasher?" you would say, "Load the dishwasher now." Or instead of saying, "Can you please be nice to your sister?" you would say, "Never antagonize your sister."

*Effective follow-through*: This refers to whatever technique you employ to ensure that your rules are followed. For example, reinforce positive behavior by thinking of the opposite of the child's negative behavior and giving your child verbal affirmation for the opposite positive behavior. If your children fight with each other, wait until they're helpful and say, "I love the way you offered to help your sister. That brings so much joy to my heart." Or allow natural consequences to occur. If your child refused to wear a jacket and then asks you to let him wear your jacket because he's cold, tell him no. Or use the "when, then" principle. When the child does what you want her to do, then you'll do what she wants you to do: "When you clean your room, then I'll drive you to your friend's house."

*Consistency*: Stay consistent with your rules. Work together as parents. Make sure both husband and wife are enforcing every rule and applying the same consequences. Tell your rules to other care-takers (coaches, teachers, and babysitters) so that your children have the same expectations across settings.

In addition to the four elements of effective discipline mentioned previously, it's important to avoid some common pitfalls of parental authority. Don't yell at your child. Proverbs reminds us all, including parents, to be gentle with our speech and to avoid reckless words that pierce like a sword (see Proverbs 12:18 and 15:1). If your child's broken a house rule, stay calm and matter of fact as you restate the rule and inform your child of the consequence. Don't provoke or shame your children as this causes them to become discouraged (see Colossians 3:21). Avoid inconsistent decisions, such as changing your no answer to yes. This encourages children to argue, pout, whine, and complain. Avoid modeling bad behavior. African American author James Baldwin wisely said, "Children have never been very good at listening to their elders, but they never failed to imitate them."[8] It's important as parents to be what we want to see.

## Our Calling as Children:
## What the Bible Says to Children

The Bible has only a few passages explicitly describing the proper relationship between children and parents. For instance, Proverbs 1:8–9 instructs children to listen to the teaching of their mother and father. Paul says in Ephesians 6:1–4, "Children, obey your parents in the Lord, for this is right. 'Honor your father and mother' (this is the first commandment with a promise), 'that it may go well with you and that you may live long in the land.'" Honor may look different for children depending on whether they're young, adolescents, and adults. For young children, it may simply be doing what your parents ask of you. For adolescents, it may involve identifying the core virtues underneath the surface request and offering a different means or strategy of living in alignment with those virtues. For adult children, it may mean respectfully declining to fulfill a parental request because it contradicts one's own core virtues.

Some of my clients wonder if it's possible to honor their parents while still maintaining healthy boundaries and living by their own core virtues. I tell them yes. Consider a client of mine whose alcoholic father demanded that he cosign on a consolidation loan because the father was in significant credit card debt due to irresponsible financial decisions and the father's credit was too poor for him to qualify for a loan on his own. I reminded my client that God disciplines those whom he loves (see Hebrews 12:6) and that the best way he could love and honor his father was to avoid enabling his father to continue to make irresponsible financial decisions. I told my client what his father really needed was for him not to cosign on a loan when the borrower (his father) was unlikely to repay the loan. Thus he could serve as a role model to his father on how to handle financial decisions wisely. On the other hand, I've had clients who've unfairly cut off their parents due to resentment. In these cases, I encourage my clients to see their parents as neither all good nor all bad and to maintain protective boundaries while participating in a limited relationship where they honor their parents by extending them forgiveness (see Matthew 18:21–22).

## The Calling of Brothers and Sisters

Scripture is also sparse on explicit admonitions on the relationship between biological brothers and sisters. One passage that directly speaks to the relationship of siblings is Genesis 4:1–18. In this well-known story of Cain and Abel, where Adam's and Eve's first child murders his younger brother, it's clear that God's call for Cain is to be his "brother's keeper." What does that mean? I would argue it means that brothers and sisters in families ought to protect, provide for, encourage, forgive, and support each other even in difficult seasons (see Proverbs 17:17). An instructive story in this regard is Joseph and his brothers in Genesis 37–50. Despite the fact that Joseph was thrown into a pit and sold into slavery by his evil brothers, Joseph didn't take revenge on them when he had the chance. After God delivered Joseph out of Egyptian slavery and prison and caused Joseph to become Pharaoh's right-hand man, Joseph's brothers came to Egypt in need from a great famine. When Joseph saw his brothers, he didn't make slaves of them even though he had the power and cause to do so. Rather, he graciously chose to love, forgive, provide for, and reconcile with his brothers (see Genesis 50:15–20).

Several biblical verses address virtues that create healthy relationships between brothers and sisters in Christ. These can readily apply by analogy to relationships between brothers and sisters in family life. Four of these virtues are described next.

*Peace*: In Matthew 5:23–24, Jesus instructs brothers and sisters to reconcile to one another before making an offering to God. This is consistent with Jesus' words in Matthew 5:9, "Blessed are the peacemakers, for they shall be called sons of God." Notice that Jesus didn't say, "Blessed are the peacekeepers." Often brothers and sisters attempt to keep peace by avoiding conflicts or denying its existence. Neither strategy is helpful. Unresolved conflict between brothers and sisters is corrosive to relational connection and must be resolved quickly through mutual understanding, empathy, humility, confession, repentance, forgiveness, and reconciliation.

*Humility*: Jesus advocated for humility when he taught his followers not to point out the speck of sawdust in the eyes of a brother or sister before they pulled the plank out of their own eyes (see Matthew 7:3–5). Brothers and sisters should confess and ask forgiveness for their own sins before pointing out each other's sins.

*Honor*: James 4:11 tells brothers and sisters not to speak evil of or slander each other. Rather, brothers and sisters should honor and respect each other with their words, actions, and attitudes (see Romans 12:10 and 1 Peter 2:17).

*Kindness*: This is the warm, authentic, and generous extension of care and compassion for others without expecting anything in return (see Colossians 3:12 and Titus 3:3–7). Kindness flows when God's love in Christ penetrates our lives and emanates from our hearts (see 1 John 4:7–11).

## Conclusion

Whether you're a husband or wife, mother or father, son or daughter, brother or sister, or boyfriend or girlfriend, the Bible and psychology provide practical guidance for preparing to live in and living in marriage and families in a virtuous and honorable manner. Dating partners should help each other grow personally and preserve one another's purity. Husbands and wives are encouraged to serve their spouse unconditionally through mutual love and respect. Marriages thrive when spouses are dedicated and committed to one another. Parents are encouraged to discipline, comfort, and provide wise counsel to their children. Children are encouraged to obey and honor their parents in accordance with their age and life stage. Brothers and sisters should protect and make peace with their siblings with humility and kindness. When a commitment is made to live out these virtues, families draw closer together, thereby fulfilling their God-given vocations in marriage and family life.

### Exercises for Reflection and Discussion

1. Make a list of five ways you can love and respect your future or current spouse. Share the list with a current spouse or a good friend of the opposite sex and ask what he or she thinks.

2. Before you date someone, what qualities do you look for in the other person? How do you want to be treated by someone you're dating?

3. Make a list of five core family virtues you plan on teaching your children to live by. What effective discipline techniques will you use to encourage and enforce each virtue?

4. Discuss with a grandparent what it means to "honor your father and your mother" (Exodus 20:12) at different stages of life. Write a prayer for God to help you honor your parent(s) at this stage of your life.

5. Identify an issue where you're keeping the peace with your sibling rather than making peace. Try to make peace by having a hard conversation where you remain humble, kind, and forgiving.

## Notes

1 William H. Quinn and Mark Odell, "Predictors of Marital Adjustment during the First Two Years," *Marriage and Family Review* 27, nos. 1–2 (1998): 113–30.

2 Linda J. Waite, Don Browning, William J. Doherty, Maggie Gallagher, Ye Luo, and Scott M. Stanley, *Does Divorce Make People Happy? Findings from a Study of Unhappy Marriages* (New York: Institute for American Values, 2002), 4.

3 Scott Stanley, Daniel Trathen, Savanna McCain, and Milt Bryan, *A Lasting Promise: The Christian Guide to Fighting for Your Marriage* (San Francisco: Jossey-Bass, 2014), 247, 251–58.

4 E. M. Waring, Betsy Schaefer, and Richard Fry, "The Influence of Therapeutic Self-Disclosure on Perceived Marital Intimacy," *Journal of Sex & Marital Therapy* 20, no. 2 (1994): 135–46.

5 Helen Fisher, *Anatomy of Love: A Natural History of Mating, Marriage, and Why We Stray* (New York: W. W. Norton, 2016), 150–51.

6 Andrew M. Greeley, *Faithful Attraction* (New York: Tor Books, 1991), 143–45.

7 Evelyn L. Lehrer and Carmel U. Chiswick, "Religion as a Determinant of Marital Stability," *Demography* 30, no. 3 (1993): 385–404.

8 James Baldwin, *Nobody Knows My Name* (1961; repr., New York: Vintage, 1993), 61–62.

# The Church

## A Call to God's Family

*Jonathan Ruehs*

### Forever a Family

The image of the family is concrete and universal. Ask anyone on the street to describe a family, and they'll describe that image in a wide variety of ways. Some will speak very positively about family. Others will describe families in negative terms. Some will describe families using biological terminology, and still others will broaden their view of family to include those who were adopted into their family. Despite how you, or others, describe a family, there's one thing for certain: you didn't make a choice to be in your family. Think about this from the perspective of biology. You didn't have a choice when it came to be being born into your family. Others made that choice for you. The same is true in adoption. Babies and young children are adopted into families regularly without them being asked if they want to be adopted. Even those who are old enough to express an opinion aren't first and foremost the ones who make the choice. It starts with a couple who wants to adopt. An older child may reject being adopted, and that might even factor into the couple deciding not to adopt the child. But that rejection doesn't negate the initial desire or drive on the part of the couple to adopt.

The point to all this is that God's church, as the eternal family of God, works in the same way. You don't choose to be in God's family; rather, God chooses you to become one of his children. For example, we read in 1 Peter 2:9 these words: "But you are a chosen race, a royal priesthood, a holy nation, a people for his own possession, that you may proclaim the excellencies of him who called you out of darkness into his marvelous light." Twice in that passage Peter uses language indicating that God chooses. In using the words *chosen race* and *his own possession*, Peter is proclaiming that becoming a member of God's family is God's work, not a human work. Peter is also echoing an ancient understanding of God's family found in the Old Testament book of Deuteronomy. We read these words from Deuteronomy 7:6–8, given to the people of ancient Israel (which included people of other nations who became a part of Israel) after God rescued them from slavery:

> For you are a people holy to the LORD your God. The LORD your God has chosen you to be a people for his treasured possession, out of all the peoples who are on the face of the earth. It was not because you were more in number than any other people that the LORD set his love on you and chose you, for you were the fewest of all people, but it is because the LORD loves you and is keeping the oath that he swore to your fathers, that the LORD has brought you out with a mighty hand and redeemed you from the house of slavery, from the hand of Pharaoh king of Egypt.

Notice what God says in Deuteronomy. His choosing Israel had nothing to do with some quality that Israel displayed; rather, it was based solely on his love for them. Peter, using the same language to describe the church in the New Testament, is making the same argument. The church doesn't choose itself; rather, God chooses the church. Just as God chose Israel based on his love, so God chooses the church based on that same love.

What is that love of God? Here's how Jesus describes that love from one of the most famous passages of the Bible, John 3:16 (NIV): "For God so loved the world that he gave his one and only Son, that whoever believes in him shall not perish but have eternal life." God's love is found concretely in Jesus—the Son of God—coming into the world. Jesus came to this world in order to enter into that darkness referenced previously in 1 Peter 2:9. The word *darkness* is synonymous with another biblical word: sin. We're born into sin. We live in it. We do it. We can't escape from sin, because it's in us. It's the spiritual pollution that's all around us. It's what darkens our hearts to do bad and evil things. It's why so many families are broken. The existence of death, Romans 6:23 tells us, is a consequence of sin. It's the payment that's due for sin. A payment that doesn't just result in physical death but, even worse, results in an eternal death. An eternal existence away from God, our loving Father.

This darkness is why Jesus came into the world. God the Father sent God the Son, Jesus, to take on our human flesh in order to live the perfect life that we can't live and to die the death that we deserve to die in order to redeem us. We encountered the word *redeem* in the Deuteronomy passage quoted previously. It means to buy back something. Jesus came to buy us out of darkness, out of our slavery to sin and death.

How did Jesus redeem us? Here's how Peter describes it in 1 Peter 1:18–19: "not with perishable things such as silver or gold, but with the precious blood of Christ." Jesus willingly entered the world's darkness in order to redeem the world. He took darkness upon himself. He became your sin. He then died in your place and redeemed you by his blood shed on a cross. The shedding of blood is indicative of a sacrifice. It's a payment of death, a pure being dying so that an impure person can live. Throughout the Old Testament we read about pure animals, such as unblemished lambs or goats, being used as substitute sacrifices (see, for instance, Leviticus 16:1–34). Instead of humans paying for their sins with their lives, God allowed, for a time, unblemished animals as substitutes. With Jesus' death on the cross, he became the "once for all" sacrifice for all people (Hebrews 9:12). No longer is there a need for animals to be sacrificed again and again. Yet death didn't have the last word in Jesus' sacrifice. If it did, then the completion of Jesus' work of redeeming us from sin and death would be incomplete. The Bible tells us that three days after his death, Jesus rose from the grave. Jesus' victory over death secured our redemption. This is the ultimate picture of the love of God, a love willing to go to the greatest lengths of sacrifice to deliver people from darkness and bring them into the light of grace. Jesus' death and resurrection bring people into the light and into God's family.

How do Jesus' death and resurrection make us a part of God's family? The Bible states that it's through both a birthing and an adoption process. How is it possible that we're both born and adopted into God's family? These are two metaphors that describe what happens in baptism. Baptism may or may not be a familiar concept to you. For those of you not familiar with baptism, it's a means whereby through water and God's Word, people are transitioned into God's family. For example, in the Gospel of John 3:3–5, we read a story about Jesus' conversation concerning entry into the Kingdom of God with a man named Nicodemus. In the midst of his conversation, Jesus tells Nicodemus that a person needs to be born again in order to come into God's Kingdom. He further describes the nature of this new birth: it happens by water and the Spirit of God. Here Jesus is describing baptism as the work of God's Spirit—the third member of the mysterious Trinity—that involves water. While Jesus doesn't explicitly describe the involvement of God's Word here, he does in Matthew 28:19 when he states that baptism is to be done in the "name of the Father and of the Son and of the Holy Spirit." The new birth that all experience in baptism is a birth into the very name of God. It means that God's name is placed upon those being baptized. It's how he designates his family. They carry the very name of God on them. It's similar to being in your own family. Your last name designates you as part of your family. So too in baptism God marks you and claims you as his own.

Being born anew into God's family also means being born into a new identity. The apostle Paul describes this new identity in this way: "I have been crucified with Christ. It is no longer I who live, but Christ who lives in me. And the life I now live in the flesh I live by faith in the Son of God, who loved me and gave himself for me" (Galatians 2:20). In baptism, we participate in Christ's death and resurrection (see Romans 6:1–4). Because Christ's redemptive work is directly and intimately imparted into our lives in baptism, we're born into a new identity in Jesus.

Adoption is the other metaphor that the Bible uses to describe being brought into God's family. Paul, in his letter to the church at Galatia, talks about it this way: "But when the fullness of time had come, God sent forth his Son, born of woman, born under the law, to redeem those who were under the law, so that we might receive adoption as [children]. And because you are [children], God has sent the Spirit of his Son into our hearts, crying, 'Abba! Father!' So you are no longer a slave, but a [child], and if a [child], then an heir through God" (Galatians 4:4–7). God adopts us out of sin and darkness. He adopts us into his family through baptism. In being adopted into God's family, we receive full rights as members of the family. This is what Paul means when he uses the word *heir*. We inherit everything that it means to be in God's family, which is to inherit God's forgiveness, grace, and an eternally good life in him. Through Christ's redeeming work, we can now call God "Father," and Christ becomes our elder brother. All believers, regardless of ethnicity, social standing, or background, become fellow brothers and sisters in the family of God in the same way.

## Saints and Sinners

In describing our status as part of God's family, the Bible describes us not only as being brothers and sisters but also as saints and priests. When we talk about saints, we first need to challenge a few misunderstandings about this term. For starters, the Bible describes both living and dead believers as saints. In regards to living people, we need only to read the opening verses of many of Paul's letters in the New Testament (see, for instance, Romans 1:7; 1 Corinthians 1:2; 2 Corinthians 1:1; Ephesians 1:1; Philippians 1:1; and Colossians 1:2). In these letters, Paul often starts off addressing living believers in Jesus as saints of God. Yet believers who have died continue in that sainthood even at death (see Psalm 116:15).

This brings us to a second misunderstanding. Sainthood isn't something that a person earns. You might have heard someone refer to another person as a "saint" because that individual was so helpful or morally good. You might have also heard someone use the phrase "Well, he's no saint" to describe someone who's questionable in his morality. Herein lies the problem: equating sainthood with morality. If sainthood is equated with morality, then sainthood is something that a person earns by good works. This is contrary to how the Bible describes saints. For example, in 1 Corinthians 1:2, Paul talks about saints this way: "To the church of God that is in Corinth, to those sanctified in Christ Jesus, called to be saints together with all those who in every place call upon the name of our Lord Jesus

Christ." According to Paul, saints are people sanctified in Christ Jesus. The verb *sanctify* means to "make holy." We also get the noun *saint* from the verb *sanctify*, which means that we can interpret the noun *saint* as a "holy one." Yet notice Paul's description of how people are sanctified. They're sanctified in Christ Jesus. Only Christ can make people holy. All this goes back to Christ's work on the cross. In taking on our darkness, our sin, he gave us his holiness, his perfection, his sinlessness. Saints are holy, but their holiness isn't their own doing. It's only and always Christ's holiness that makes them that way. Finally, notice how Paul states that saints are called. The notion of being called takes us back to how we're brought into God's family. It's God's work that makes us saints, not our own work. God calls us into this life through Christ and by his Spirit. We neither initiate this calling to sainthood nor choose it.

At this point, you still might be leery of "saint" language. You might think, "Well, if Christians are saints, and Christ made them that way, then why do they still sometimes act like sinners?" It's truly unfortunate that Christians behave badly from time to time and even engage in some heinous acts. Understand that God doesn't intend or condone these acts. For example, God didn't condone the so-called holy wars that have occurred between Christians and Muslims. Nor does God condone church leaders today who use their position to mistreat and sexually abuse others. Yet the Bible describes that while Christians are saints, they also continue to wrestle with sin. As an example, we turn to Romans 7:19–20 and read Paul's description of his own wrestling with sin: "For I do not do the good I want, but the evil I do not want is what I keep on doing. Now if I do what I do not want, it is no longer I who do it, but sin that dwells within me." In exasperation, Paul declares, "Wretched man that I am! Who will deliver me from this body of death?" (Romans 7:24). Paul quickly gives us the answer in the next verse: it's Jesus who rescues!

Christians will continue to wrestle with this inner warfare between the saint and the sinner until either they breathe their last breath or Christ comes again. When Jesus comes again, this warfare will be brought to an end. The sinner-saint will become a fully glorified saint—a completely new creation in body, soul, and mind (see 1 Corinthians 15:35–58)—who no longer struggles with sin. While this side of the resurrection is a wearying battle, and many times

Christians are tempted to give in and give up, it's nevertheless a holy battle to engage in because it's a fight between the old sinful self and the new life in Jesus. So while Christians do live out their sainthood and show compassion, mercy, and forgiveness to others—a reflection of the holiness of Jesus—they also sometimes commit hypocritical acts that reflect the darkness within. What this means is that the church as a family will sometimes act in dysfunctional ways by arguing, engaging in power plays, and doing all manner of ugly things. This is why one of the greatest marks of the church is forgiveness. Forgiveness is rooted in and reflects the love and mercy that believers have received from Christ for their sins (see Colossians 3:12–13 and 1 John 4:7–11). Forgiveness completely absolves others who've wronged them—even seriously so—and seeks to create loving relationships where there was once apathy or hostility.

This forgiveness differs from the forgiveness shown in the world. The world's forgiveness is limited and contractual. It draws a line in the sand and says, "I'll only go this far and no farther." It says things like, "I'll only forgive if you do this for me." Maybe this is why when someone wrongs another person the wrongdoer tends to say "I'm sorry" as opposed to "Will you forgive me?" Notice the difference between the statement and the question. The person apologizing is still in control, whereas asking for forgiveness relinquishes control. True forgiveness is about giving up power. It's the recognition that you can't pardon yourself; rather, the person you've sinned against is the one who decides to pardon you. It can be difficult to give up power and to place the decision to be pardoned into another person's hands. For example, when someone has gossiped and defamed another person's character, that person rightly seeks justice. The victim wants the wrong to be righted. When the guilty party—in this case, the gossiper—comes forward and seeks forgiveness, he places power over his life into the hands of the wronged party, hoping to be pardoned. He's asking that no retributive action be taken against him and that he be given a clean slate with all wrongdoing erased. Forgiveness isn't easy to give, especially in the face of deep or persistent wrongdoing. This is why our forgiveness must be connected to God's forgiveness. If we seek to forgive someone out of our own reservoir of mercy, then forgiveness won't come. To forgive out of the poverty of one's heart is like trying to quench thirst by consuming desert sand. The flood of God's forgiveness for us flows into our lives and out of our hearts so that complete, unconditional forgiveness pours out of us and into those who've wronged us.

The world's limited forgiveness and the church's complete forgiveness are illustrated in Peter's conversation with Jesus recorded in Matthew 18:21–22. Peter asks Jesus how often he should forgive someone who sins against him. Peter asks if forgiving someone up to seven times is enough, most likely thinking that this is generous. Jesus tells him that he should forgive that person not "seven times, but seventy-seven times." Jesus' number is hyperbolic. He's indicating that the forgiveness Peter is to show is to be unqualified and never-ending. Because forgiveness is at the heart of God, it's also at the heart of the church and its saints. It's the lifeblood, so to speak, of the church's existence and work in the world. It's why the church gathers each week to worship together. Christians need to hear the good news of God's forgiveness for them regularly. It's why Paul starts many of his letters to the early Christian churches telling them about God's forgiveness (see, for instance, Ephesians 1:1–10). Without the forgiveness of God, the life of faith and forgiveness wouldn't exist at all.

## Priests

We've talked about the word *saint*, but what does it mean to be a priest? Like saint, the word *priest* is a loaded term. You might think of a Catholic priest as someone who's wearing a clerical collar or maybe dressed in robes. Or you might think about tribal priests in African religions. Folks whose job it is to offer sacrifices to appease the gods/goddesses of that faith. The word *priest* in the Bible carries similar connotations. In the Old Testament, we read how God called a particular tribe, the Levities, to be priests who bring sacrifices of atonement to God on behalf of the whole nation of Israel (see Numbers 18:1–32). Atonement means "covering." The goal in atonement is for a person's or a nation's sins to be covered over, in other words, to be forgiven. How are a person's sins covered in the sacrifice of atonement? As talked about previously concerning redemption, it's done by substituting in death one who's pure for the morally impure so that the innocent one bears the penalty of sin for others and, in turn, they're forgiven and live. Sin brings with it the penalty of death. It's the demand of justice. As humans, we understand the demands of justice. When we've been the recipients of an unjust act, we cry out for justice. Our demands for justice are an imperfect echo of God's demands for justice. God demands justice for the sins that we commit. As Psalm 51:4 says, all sin against God. Even the sins that we do to another person (e.g., lying, stealing, murdering) are ultimately sins against God, since we're acting unjustly toward God's creation.

God is perfectly just, yet he's also perfectly loving. So in his mercy toward us, God provides another way for us to pay the debt that justice demands. In the Old Testament, the atonement for sins was accomplished by substituting sinners with an animal. For example, in the annual Day of Atonement ritual described in Leviticus 16:1–34, a goat was picked to act as the pure substitute for all of impure Israel. The goat's blood was shed in place of Israel. But atoning sacrifices didn't just happen once a year. An Israelite could have the priests make a sacrifice on his behalf anytime he needed. You could say the work of the priest was a bloody mess.

When we switch to the New Testament, we read of the final atoning work of Christ for all of humanity. Jesus was the perfect, sinless Lamb of God who was sacrificed for everyone upon the altar of the cross (see John 1:29; 2 Corinthians 5:21; and Hebrews 2:17–18). God, in the greatest act of love and mercy, sent his own Son to be that final atoning sacrifice. In this way, God met his demands of justice. Not only was Jesus the sacrifice, but he also served as the priest, since he was the one who offered himself as the sacrifice.

So how does all this relate to our calling as priests? Recall the words from 1 Peter 2:9 quoted at the beginning of this chapter. Peter talks about how God's people are to be a "royal priesthood." The office of the priesthood, according to Peter, isn't limited to one individual or a certain tribe of people. All Christians are called to serve as priests. The reason all Christians are called as priests is because of Jesus serving as our Great High Priest. He did the once-for-all work of atonement on our behalf, which enables believers to engage in priestly work for others in response.

What does this priestly work look like? Since there's no need for bloody sacrifices to be made because Christ was the last and ultimate sacrifice, Christians are called to engage in a different type of sacrificial work. Paul speaks about the sacrificial work of Christians in Romans 12:1, where he writes, "I appeal to you therefore, brothers, by the mercies of God, to present your bodies as a living sacrifice, holy and acceptable to God, which is your spiritual worship." What does Paul mean by this? As theologian Paul Althaus explains, "We stand before God, pray for others, intercede with and sacrifice ourselves to God and proclaim the word [of the gospel] to one another. . . . The Christian's priestly sacrifice is nothing else than Christ's own sacrifice."[1] But unlike the work of Christ, the sacrificial acts of Christians aren't for atonement—theirs or others. Rather, they're responsive acts of thanksgiving to Christ's atoning work for them. Neither is Christian compassion—giving food to the homeless or money to the poor, tutoring orphans, donating blood, or whatever—for gaining God's favor or raising one's image in the eyes of others. Christian compassion focuses on others, on helping one's neighbors. It doesn't look for people's praise; rather, it wants people to see Christ, who works through Christians' priestly acts of sacrifice.

In acting as priests, Christians are acting like Jesus. The identity of Jesus, the Great High Priest, is imprinted upon Christians in their baptisms, as Paul points out: "Do you not know that all of us who have been baptized into Christ Jesus were baptized into his death? We were buried therefore with him by baptism into death, in order that, just as Christ was raised from the dead by the glory of the Father, we too might walk in newness of life. For if we have been united with him in a death like his, we shall certainly be united with him in a resurrection like his" (Romans 6:3–5). Through baptism, the Christian life reflects the sacrifice of the Great High Priest for all people. What this means is that as someone encounters a Christian, they're encountering the crucified and risen Lord! So when Christians proclaim forgiveness to others, it's the forgiveness of Christ they receive. When Christians offer up prayers on behalf of others, it's Christ who offers up those prayers interceding to the Father for them (see Hebrews 7:23–25). When Christians provide words of comfort or a shoulder to cry on, it's Christ who's offering them that comfort. When Christians make a personal sacrifice to help others, it's Christ who humbles himself to serve their needs.

It might be hard for people to see these priestly actions of Jesus in sinful human beings. They see the bad and the ugly in the life of Christians, which might cloud them from seeing the good in Christian lives. Again, we recall the previous words concerning the dual nature of Christians as saint and sinner. It's also important to recall Paul's words in Colossians 3:1–4, where he states, "If then you have been raised with Christ, seek the things that are above, where Christ is, seated at the right hand of God. Set your minds on things that are above, not on things that are on earth. For you have died, and your life is hidden with Christ in God. When Christ who is your life appears, then you also will appear with him in glory." As Paul makes evident, the true life of the Christian is a hidden life. This doesn't mean that Christ doesn't shine through that person, but prior to Christ's second coming—when all saints will receive imperishable bodies and natures that fully bear the image of Christ (see 1 Corinthians 15:42–49)—that life won't be completely revealed. It's a convoluted life and yet a life that's still secured in Christ.

This is why when we look at Christian history, we can see wonderfully compassionate Christian acts done in the name of Jesus. The first hospitals and orphanages were started and developed by Christians out of the compassion that Christ showed for the poor, sick, and needy in his own life. Christians in the early church were the first to oppose slavery in Roman society, denouncing it as a sin against the common humanity and equal rights people have by being created in God's image. Some Christians even sold themselves as slaves to redeem others from slavery. Centuries later, antislavery movements in the New World were mostly led by Christians.[2] In the twentieth century, Mother Teresa gave her life to be the hands and feet of Christ among the poor in Kolkata, India. This work continues to this day with the Missionaries of Charity, even after her death. These are just a few examples of baptized believers in Jesus working sacrificially in the world.

Yet that same glowing Christian history also has an unfortunate dark side. As Christianity grew in prominence in Europe, it eventually became the dominant religion of the various empires there. As those empires branched out into other parts of the world, they sought to conquer and colonize new lands in the name of their kings and in the name of Jesus. For example, when galleons reached the New World, they brought not only soldiers with them but priests as well. Unfortunately, the work of evangelizing indigenous people wasn't always done by the Spirit but by the point of the sword.

The Christian church celebrates the compassionate acts done in the past and into the present, giving thanks to God for the work that he does in and through his people. Yet the church also needs to repent of horrific acts that have been done and still are done in the name of Jesus. Priestly work, in this regard, involves bringing others to repentance over such evil acts and returning to God, who not only convicts people of their sins but also showers upon them mercy and forgiveness.

## Invited and Inviting into God's Family

You may have heard it said that God is the Father of all people. This makes sense when you see that God creates everyone and provides for them. It's also sensible, since God desires to include all people in his eternal family through his Son, Jesus. Regardless of the sinful lives that they have led, people of all backgrounds and walks of life are welcomed into God's family. Rich and poor alike have equal access. People from America to Zimbabwe—and all countries of the alphabet in-between—are invited.

God freely offers his gift of grace to everyone. But if people don't want it, then they can reject it. Even though God desires all people to be saved (see 1 Timothy 2:4), God doesn't force his Fatherhood upon anyone. For people to reject God as Father, though, means to reject his love, forgiveness, and grace for their lives. It means that they'll have to face God as judge. Not as someone whose judgment has already been taken care of by Christ but as someone who has rejected that "not guilty" verdict and decided to face God on his or her own terms.

This is why Christians want to share their faith with other people. In the words of the Sri Lankan evangelist D. T. Niles, "Christianity is one beggar telling another beggar where he found bread."[3] Christians are spiritual beggars who've found the "bread of life" that is Jesus (John 6:35). Christians shouldn't horde Jesus to themselves, concerned that he's only enough bread for them; rather, as the Bread of Life, he's more than enough for all. Jesus demonstrates this in a well-known miracle, the feeding of the five thousand. In the Gospel of John, we read the story of Jesus taking five little loaves of bread and two little fish and miraculously reproducing more than enough food for all the people gathered. Note what John says about this feast: "Jesus then took the loaves, and when he had given thanks, he distributed them to those who were seated. So also the fish, as much as they wanted. And when they had eaten their fill, he told his disciples, 'Gather up the leftover fragments, that nothing may be lost.' So they gathered them up and filled twelve baskets with fragments from the five barley loaves left by those who had eaten" (John 6:11–13). John states that the people could eat as much as they wanted and the leftovers filled twelve large baskets. This is the context behind Jesus telling the people that he's the Bread of Life. If Jesus could easily take care of their temporary needs such that everyone was full with plenty of leftovers, then he can certainly take care of everyone's eternal needs without anyone going spiritually hungry.

God seeks to save everyone, adopting them as his children through the atoning work of his Son, Jesus Christ. God invites all people into his eternal family. A family that includes sanctified people—saints—from every nation, class, and generation (see Galatians 3:26–28 and Revelation 7:9–10).

## Exercises for Reflection and Discussion

1. What words come to mind when you hear the word *Christian*? Explain why those were the first things you thought of.
2. How does a person become a member of God's family? Share two or three points from this chapter with a partner that help you answer this question.
3. What is one of the most heinous acts that one person can do against another person? Is that act ever unforgiveable in the eyes of the Christian faith? Why or why not?
4. Take a sheet of paper and draw a line across the middle. On the upper half of the paper, jot down some words that describe your identity. Next to each word, draw a picture or write a

sentence that explains how that identity influences the way you think about the world, feel about yourself, or act toward others. On the bottom half, write the words *saint* and *priest*. Reflect on what those identities mean. Explain how being a saint and priest might change the way you think, feel, or act.

## Notes

1 Paul Althaus, *The Theology of Martin Luther*, trans. Robert C. Schultz (1966; repr., Philadelphia: Fortress, 1970), 314–15.

2 For the philosophical premises of slavery in the Western world and its Christian opposition, see Korey D. Maas, "Christianity's Cultural Legacy," in *Making the Case for Christianity: Responding to Modern Objections*, ed. Korey D. Maas and Adam S. Francisco (St. Louis: Concordia, 2014), 177–87.

3 Quoted in David Black, "The Callings," *New York Times*, May 11, 1986, accessed June 23, 2019, https://www.nytimes.com/1986/05/11/magazine/the-callings.html.

# The Vocation of Friendship

## A Disruptive and Healing Force

*John Norton*

## A High Calling

The vocation of friendship is a blessing God uses to transform every-day life. Friends can have a massive influence on the way we see and on the way we act. The vocation of friendship is demanding and must be engaged thoughtfully and humbly. As contemporary scholar Gene Veith writes in his book *God at Work*, the concept of vocation reminds us that every kind of work is an opportunity "for exercising a holy service to God and to one's neighbor."[1] Veith's terminology about vocation helps us recognize that God's friendship "looms behind" our human friendships.[2] Considering friendship as a vocation will elevate our understanding of this important role—a role that many have mistaken for a simple diversion. In *The Four Loves*, literature scholar C. S. Lewis explains that in the ancient world, friendship was regarded as the "happiest and most fully human of all loves; the crown of life and the school of virtue."[3] Lewis claims that friendship alone—more than affection, romantic love, or uncondi-tional love—raises us "to the level of gods or angels [and must be regarded as] a relation between men at their highest level of individ-uality."[4] I share Lewis's goal of urging readers to see friendship with new eyes—to see the vocation of friendship as a high calling that involves not only great challenges but also great blessings.

Friendship was created by God for our good. The sixteenth-century theologian Martin Luther taught that God's goodness is illustrated in his knowledge and care of human need: "For it is natural—and everybody must admit this—that everyone would like to be shown love, fidelity, and help. Therefore we have been intermingled by God [in friendships and other relationships] in order that we may live side by side and serve and help one another."[5] This high calling to friendship mustn't cause us to draw back in fear but rather to "'dare something' in the name of Christ," as theologian Matthew Harrison encourages us in his book *Christ Have Mercy*.[6] In this text, Harrison addresses the natural human inclination to wilt before the high call of God, yet grace guides us forward. Harrison writes, "The mission for mercy is before us all, and so is our Lord. It is time for the 'demons' that have caused us to lose courage for the day to be exorcized, and what was spoken once to a demon-possessed man is now spoken of us, 'Go home to your friends and tell them how much the Lord has done for you, and how He has had mercy on you.'"[7] Harrison's encouragement is to serve and love our friends courageously. The vocation of friendship is not only one we must recognize as important and challenging but also one that God will equip us to engage as we trust him. May this chapter reveal friendship as a gift from God that offers mercy in the form of faithful disruption and deep healing.

## What Is Friendship?

No serious chapter on friendship could be complete without mention of those powerful arbiters of relational wisdom—the Spice Girls. In their 1997 chart-topping hit "Wannabe," these pop giants offer compelling ideas about friendship in a tune that makes even an old, tired professor jump out of his chair. The chorus of the song reads as follows:

> If you wanna be my lover, you gotta get with my friends
> Make it last forever friendship never ends
> If you wanna be my lover, you have got to give
> Taking is too easy, but that's the way it is[8]

While the phrase "get with" has some muddy connotations, the over-all message is clear and strong—friends matter. Friends, as related by the Spice Girls, are part of one's identity; they're part of what makes people "who they are." It may come as a bit of surprise that a band made up of nicknames like Scary Spice, Sporty Spice, Baby Spice, Ginger Spice, and Posh Spice would be tapping into classical ideas to form their biggest hit, but facts are facts.

In Greece in 350 BC, the philosopher Aristotle wrote that a man is related to his friend as he is to himself, "for his friend is another self."[9] It's not known if Aristotle wrote these ideas as part of a lyrical demand to his wife, Pythias, but we can see some clear connections between the ancient Greek scholarship and the twentieth-century pop song. The Spice Girls want their lovers to approve of their friends and to recognize that their friends are connected and important, like another self.

Another potential influence for the Spice Girls may be found in ancient Rome where, in 44 BC, the philosopher Cicero praised friendship as something strong and deeply personal. Cicero wrote, "But in friendship there is nothing feigned, nothing pretended, and whatever there is in it is both genuine and spontaneous. Friendship, therefore, springs from nature rather than from need,—from an inclination of the mind with a certain consciousness of love rather than from calculation of the benefit to be derived from it."[10] Matching Cicero's emphasis on nature and spontaneity, the Spice Girls did *not* sing, "If you wanna be my lover, you gotta get with my business partners or my network." In the spirit of friendship that Cicero describes in his book *De Amicitia*, friendship doesn't spring from the calculated benefits demanded of business partners. Need isn't a vital part of friendship for Cicero but instead a "consciousness of love." Cicero seems to press his reader to see a difference between love and self-interest. Love, as Cicero describes, is rooted in trust and in self-sacrifice. In his book on friends, Cicero includes a few powerful lines from a popular Roman poet named Ennius to emphasize the close, unselfish bond of a friend:

"How can life be worth living, if devoid
Of the calm trust reposed by friend in friend?

What sweeter joy than in the kindred soul?
Whose converse differs not from self-communion?"[11]

Ennius connects the nouns *calm* and *trust* with the verb *repose* in order to communicate an important interdependency. *Calm* and *repose*, two words that seem nearly synonymous with *peace* and *rest*, rely on a valued sense of trust, according to Ennius. In other words, among friends who trust one another, there's a significant calm or confidence. A true friend offers peace through trusted devotion, and thus a good friend improves the value of one's life. Ennius's final question builds on the value of a friend by drawing together "converse" and "self-communion." It's here that Ennius, Cicero, and Aristotle come together even more closely. Ennius here makes a connection between the conversation one has with a trusted friend and the very thoughts that exist in one's own heart and mind.

## Friends of God

Moving forward with this conception of friendship as personal, loving, and unselfish, it's helpful to examine the words of Jesus Christ recorded in the New Testament. The teachings of Jesus have had a profound influence on the formation of Western civilization, and perhaps most powerfully on the Western concept of friendship and love. The Gospel of John records Jesus teaching the following: "Greater love has no one than this, that someone lay down his life for his friends. You are my friends if you do what I command you. No longer do I call you servants, for the servant does not know what his master is doing; but I have called you friends, for all that I have heard from my Father I have made known to you" (John 15:13–15). Jesus' conception of friendship bears some similarities to that of Aristotle and Cicero. Friendship is a personal bond that's forged through a recognition of dignity and value in the friend. Furthermore, as expressed by Jesus, the bond of friendship is proven through self-sacrifice for others, even for those who do evil and are thus currently enemies of God (see Romans 5:6–11). There's no room for demands or self-centered gain in Jesus' conception of friendship. As one would fight for his own survival or well-being, he would also fight for the survival and well-being of a friend. Jesus' ideas connect with Cicero's regarding the "genuine and the spontaneous" as he explains the oneness of mission and vision he shares with his disciples. Jesus' declaration "No longer do I call you servants" signals an important shift as he establishes a more intimate bond of friendship. Jesus signals a relational change when he calls the disciples his friends. Their relationship is no longer to be compared to masters and slaves, or employers and employees. One of the most powerful elements in Jesus' teaching encourages us that one's love of a friend may equal or even surpass one's love of self.

Luther claims that the friendship Christ describes in John 15 is a powerful elevation of the disciples' status. Luther writes, "Christ is exceedingly friendly, and His words are full of kindness. As He bids His disciples farewell, He urges them to take this commandment to heart, and He fixes in their minds the example which shows them how He loved them and what He did for them. . . . Christ giving His life for you. . . . This is surely the greatest love that one man on earth can show another."[12] Luther describes Christ's extension of friendship to the disciples as an act of immense kindness and as an act of great humility. That the God of the universe would humble himself by becoming a friend to sinners is outrageous. Luther builds a case for the right and proper response to this outrageous grace and to this amazing love. Luther continues with this encouragement: "It is surely kind and pleasing that Christ calls them His friends. For He would like to encourage and rouse us to pay heed to His love, to consider how He made the Father our Friend and how He proved Himself our Friend above all friends. But all of us who are His friends must also live in friendship with one another."[13] Luther is careful to explain that we don't earn our salvation by acts of sacrifice in friendship to one another, but we extend friendship to one another out of respect for Christ. Christ tells us to love one another and to join together in bonds of sacrificial friendship for our own sake and for our collective benefit.

Theologian Dietrich Bonhoeffer works with this same idea in his 1939 book *Life Together*. Bonhoeffer writes, "When God was merciful to us, we learned to be merciful with our brethren. When we received forgiveness instead of judgement, we, too, were made ready to forgive our brethren. What God [through Christ] did to us, we then owe to others."[14] The "brotherly love" (*philadelphia* in 1 Thessalonians 4:9) that God reveals in Christ is related to, but different from, friendship (*philos*) in the classical world. The idea of friendship we see described in the Bible extends to all others, echoing the reconciling love and mercy God has shown us.

Our invitation to be friends of God is a gracious affirmation of our dignity and worth. We receive this dignity because we're God's beloved children made whole and righteous by Christ's life, death, and resurrection for us. We can enter into the vocation of friendship with all people freely and courageously because we're empowered and secured by the bonds of divine friendship. These elements of the Christian view of friendship, which requires a prior reconciliation and friendship with God, marks a significant difference from Aristotle and Cicero, for whom friendship is the means of practicing certain virtues, such as temperance, prudence, and justice.

## The Practice of Friendship

In addition to demonstrating the great depth and classic weight of the Spice Girls' song lyrics, this chapter has connected conceptions of friendship as espoused by Aristotle, Cicero, and Jesus. Each of these figures emphasizes the depth of friendship and the fact that friends value each other as they value themselves. What we haven't yet begun to explore, however, are the more specific elements involved in a friend's sacrificial love. What does the vocation of friendship look like in practice?

An examination of friendship in Shakespeare's *King Lear* will be helpful in this new exploration. Shakespeare's greatest tragedy opens upon a stage swirling with confusion over the king's controversial decision. The king declares that he wants to retire and to give one portion of his kingdom to each of his three daughters, the largest portion going to the young lady who best proclaims her love for him. Lear puts it this way:

> Which of you shall we say doth love us most,
> That we our largest bounty may extend

Where nature doth with merit challenge? Goneril,
Our eldest born, speak first. (1.1.51–54)[15]

This famous scene is called "the love test," and as the reader can imagine, it doesn't end well. King Lear's two eldest daughters, Goneril and
Regan, don't hesitate to accept the king's challenge, and they proceed
to shower him with flattering professions of love and affirmation.
They see great personal gain in this moment and hope to win the
largest share of the kingdom by out-praising each other. The young-
est daughter, Cordelia, however, refuses to use her love for her father
for personal gain. Cordelia acts as a friend to her father when she
responds to him with truth and not with the tricks of flattery:

Good my Lord,
You have begot me, bred me, loved me. I
Return those duties back as are right fit,
Obey you, love you, and most honor you.
Why have my sisters husbands, if they say
They love you all? (1.1.96–100)

For clarification, we're working with a classical understanding of friendship that includes a wide range of potential partners, including daughters and fathers. According to David Konstan, professor of ancient
Greco-Roman literature, Aristotle's conception of friendship (*philos*)
made room for "parents, brothers, benefactors, fellow-tribesmen
and fellow-citizens as well as husbands and wives, fellow-voyagers,
comrades-in-arms, guest-friends, and cousins."[16] While the vocation
of a daughter is different from the vocation of a friend, the most potent
interactions Cordelia has with her father are best understood and ana-
lyzed in the context of friendship.

Instead of entering into the love test with a deposit of dramatic
flattery like her sisters, Cordelia tells the truth. She doesn't refuse her
father love, and in these lines, she communicates her affection for
him in strength and in clarity: "I obey you, love you, and most honor
you." She doesn't, however, overdramatize or flatter her father with
lies. Her truth-telling is an act of self-sacrifice, as she believes that it
would be unjust and unkind to manipulate her father for personal
gain. She asks an obvious question that should alert her father to her

sisters' deception: "Why have my sisters husbands, if they say / They love you all?" Cordelia applies logic to her profession of truth, yet her father doesn't hear her.

Lear is very upset and offended by her refusal to compete for the larger piece of the kingdom and asks, "So young, and so untender?" (1.1.106). Her response, "So young, my lord, and true" (1.1.107), illustrates her commitment to a classical and Christ-like understanding of friendship. Cordelia acts in a way toward her father that's consistent with her convictions, and she's willing to lose a kingdom to be a true friend to her father. Cordelia's decision stirs her father into a rage, and he disowns her with this oath-like declaration:

> Let it be so! Thy truth then be thy dower,
> For, by the sacred radiance of the sun,
> The mysteries of Hecate and the night,
> By all the operation of the orbs
> From whom we do exist and cease to be,
> Here I disclaim all my paternal care,
> Propinquity, and property of blood,
> And as a stranger to my heart and me
> Hold thee from this forever. (1.1.108–116)

Lear's declaration is important to consider as it reveals the great weight of the relational connection. Lear expected something different from his favorite daughter, and his words in this passage convey what seems like shock in addition to violent disappointment. When Lear disowns his daughter for speaking the truth, he officially cancels a vocation she didn't choose for herself. Ironically, it's in her chosen role as friend to Lear that Cordelia ultimately saves his life. Cordelia is also surprised and moved with sorrow at her father's decision, but she stays committed to her path. Later in the scene, she unpacks more of her conviction about how words and actions must remain closely aligned, and she voices concern about the "oily art" that her sisters have performed (1.1.228). While the term *oily art* is really nice, a more contemporary description of her sisters would include words like *slick, cagey, slippery,* or *cunning.* Cordelia sees disaster coming for her father, and as an unselfish friend, cast in a classical mold, she seeks to move him out of harm's way. Although Lear doesn't listen to

Cordelia and instead banishes her from the kingdom, the interaction between father and daughter reveals some important ideas about the practice of friendship.

## Friendship as a Disruptive Force

A friend, as understood in classical terms and as exemplified by Cordelia, is one who serves as both a disruptive force and a healing force. Aristotle argues that a "training in virtue" is one of the fruits of true friendship.[17] Aristotle presses this point and claims that a man who hopes to be happy will need virtuous friends. Cicero weighs in on the same idea; he writes, "It is virtue itself that produces and sustains friendship, not without virtue can friendship by any possibility exist."[18] It's within this argument for virtue that Cicero defends the idea that a true friend serves as a disruptive force. Cicero claims that we must be free to speak truth to a friend, "for friends often need to be admonished and reproved."[19] Truth can be disruptive and difficult to accept, but according to Cicero, uncritical satisfaction that accepts error and inaccuracy "suffers a friend to go headlong to ruin."[20] Bonhoeffer, again in *Life Together*, cites the apostle Paul's letter to the Galatians as support for the importance of the disruptive goodness of friends: "Brothers and sisters, if someone is caught in a sin, you who live by the Spirit should restore that person gently" (Galatians 6:1 NIV). Bonhoeffer argues that this line from Galatians is meant to create strong bonds of friendship through the sharing of truth. Bonhoeffer writes, "If we cannot bring ourselves to utter [the truth], we shall have to ask ourselves whether we are not still seeing our brother garbed in his human dignity which we are afraid to touch, and thus forgetting the most important thing, that he, too, no matter how old or highly placed or distinguished he may be, is still a man like us, a sinner in crying need of God's grace. He has the same great necessities that we have, and needs help, encouragement, and forgiveness as we do."[21] Bonhoeffer adds something important to our presentation of the vocation of friendship—a true friend acts in a disruptive way because he empathizes with and holds a deep respect for the God-given dignity of his friend. The truth, no matter how disruptive,

must be spoken to those we love and serve as friends. The disruptive force of a good friend, as Bonhoeffer writes, must always be
employed with great humility: "We speak to one another on the
basis of the help we both need. . . . We warn one another against
the disobedience that is our common destruction."[22] We see this
kind of humility in Cordelia's character when she refuses to play
along with the "love test" and instead speaks truth.

Cordelia seeks to disrupt her father, to stop him from rushing
"headlong to ruin" with his poorly constructed retirement plans.
She's unwilling to simply play along with a test that she believes will
lead the king to put trust in empty flatterers who will abuse him.
Cordelia disrupts the order established by her friend and father, and
in so doing, she is able to shake him up. It's clear that Cordelia understands the danger of those who pretend friendship by pouring out
flattery. She distances herself from her sisters when she sarcastically
refers to them as "jewels" (1.1.272). Cordelia accuses them publicly
with this exclamation:

> I know you what you are,
> And like a sister am most loath to call
> Your faults as they are named. Love well our father.
> To your professed bosoms I commit him,
> But yet, alas, stood I within his grace,
> I would prefer him to a better place. (1.1.273–278)

Cordelia, once again, doesn't fear speaking the truth. She knows
her sisters well; they're cunning, flattering, experts in "oily art," and
despicable. While Goneril and Regan profess to hold their father
dear, Cordelia knows that their words are empty and meaning-
less. She knows that her sisters' promises won't be upheld with any
substantial or supportive action and that they won't treat him well.
Cordelia's final words in this conversation betray a fierce commitment to the vocation of friendship. If she were still in her father's
court, able to counsel him and care for him, she wouldn't want him
in the company of her sisters but rather in "a better place." She knows
that the truth will be revealed in time, and instead of seeking immediate gain through flattery, she humbles herself beneath the truth.
Cordelia says,

> Time shall unfold what plighted cunning hides;
> Who covers faults, at last with shame derides. (1.1.284–285)

As a friend cast in the classical form, Shakespeare's Cordelia isn't only virtuously disruptive, but she's also a healing force. After Lear banishes her from the court, Cordelia travels to France with her new husband. Late in the play, at the very end of act four, the chaos of Lear's foolish decisions unfolds. It's made clear to the audience that Cordelia's time in France was spent in raising an army. She returns to England with French forces and rescues her father. By the time she lands, the king has been severely abused by her sisters and thrown out of the castle. He's been living in a cave in the woods, and his health is very poor. Cordelia orders a doctor to tend to Lear, and she prays for him, revealing her healing intent:

> O you kind gods,
> Cure this great breach in his abused nature!
> The untuned and jarring senses, O, wind up
> Of this child-changed father! (4.7.14–17)

Rage and revenge could be justified by Cordelia, for she was unkindly and unjustly banished from her father's kingdom. Lear, full of blind ignorance, threw her away in preference for Cordelia's oily tongued sisters. As a true friend, Cordelia seeks not revenge but rather healing for her father. From the initiation of the love test, Cordelia has been aware of a "great breach" in her father's nature. This breach is a disconnection from health and sanity, a separation of Lear's mind from clear sense and understanding. She prays that his "untuned and jarring senses"—his broken mind and his faltering reason—would "wind up" or recollect and heal. Cordelia calls Lear "child-changed" because his adult children Goneril and Regan "changed" him with abuse and cruelty. Cordelia adds a kiss to her prayer and speaks these tender words:

> O my dear Father! Restoration hang
> Thy medicine on my lips, and let this kiss
> Repair those violent harms that my two sisters
> Have in thy reverence made! (4.7.26–29)

As a woman of action, one whose words match her behavior, Cordelia returns to England to fight for her father's restoration and to bring the healing power of a true friend. Although in this scene Lear's mind is still deeply troubled, he sees and recognizes Cordelia, and he wonders why she isn't hurtling accusations at him. He expects something very different from her, and he kneels before her with this confession, "I am a very foolish fond old man" (4.7.61). Cordelia begs him not to kneel, and she begins to cry. With new vision and what seems a healed heart and mind, Lear apologizes and offers himself to Cordelia in humble repentance:

> Be your tears wet? Yes, faith. I pray, weep not.
> If you have poison for me I will drink it.
> I know you do not love me, for your sisters
> Have, as I do remember, done me wrong.
> You have some cause, they have not. (4.7.73–77)

Lear offers Cordelia his life. He knows he has wronged her, and part of his healing is evidenced by his repentance and humility before her. Unaware of her true feelings, however, Lear assumes that Cordelia doesn't love him. He admits that because of his foolish actions, she has good reason to hate him. Her response, "No cause, no cause" (4.7.78), serves as a healing forgiveness, and from here, we see Lear continue to grow clearer, stronger, and more aware of Cordelia's love for him.

Cordelia, as a true friend to her father, serves as a disruptive force, allowing herself to be banished for the sake of truth. She doesn't simply walk away from her father but pursues him with the healing grace of forgiveness. Cicero's description of true friendship as a healing force sounds quite a bit like Cordelia's care for Lear. Cicero writes,

> But friendship combines the largest number of utilities. Wherever you turn, it is at hand. No place shuts it out. It is never unseasonable, never annoying. Thus, as the proverb says, "You cannot put water or fire to more uses than friendship serves." I am not now speaking of the common and moderate type of friendship, which yet yields both pleasure and profit, but, of true and perfect friendship, like that which

existed in the few instances that are held in special remembrance. . . . [Friendship] certainly has this special prerogative, that it lights up a good hope for the time to come, and thus preserves the minds that it sustains from imbecility or prostration in misfortune.[23]

Cicero uses the term *utilities* to capture a broad view of friendship and to speak of its great practical value. He describes the fact that friendship is "at hand" but not "annoying." These qualities speak of a persistence and a determination that we see in Shakespeare's characterization of Cordelia. Lear banishes her, but she refuses to be shut out while, at the same time, she isn't "unseasonable" or rude. Cordelia's expression of friendship to her father heals him with a new sense of hope and draws him from the "imbecility" or foolishness caused by his own errors in judgment. Cordelia's Christ-like pursuit of her father is one of love and forgiveness, and it results in his confession.

In *Life Together*, Bonhoeffer describes the healing vocation that God has given to friends in Christ. He cites the Gospel of John as he builds his case for the healing power of a virtuous friend: "If you forgive the sins of any, they are forgiven them; if you withhold forgiveness from any, it is withheld" (John 20:23). Bonhoeffer unpacks the idea in the following lines, where I suggest that we read "friend" whenever Bonhoeffer uses "brother": "Christ became our brother in order to help us. Through him, our brother has become Christ for us in the power and authority of the commission Christ has given to him. Our brother stands before us as the sign of the truth and the grace of God. He has been given to us to help us. He hears the confession of our sins in Christ's stead and he forgives our sins in Christ's name. He keeps the secret of our confession as God keeps it."[24] Cordelia's pursuit of her father, bearing the healing forgiveness of a true friend, results in his confession. It's in Lear's confession that we see his healing most powerfully illustrated.

Shakespeare creates his character Cordelia with an extraordinary measure of courage and unselfishness. She's like Christ to her father, giving her own life for his sake and thus providing us with a vivid example of faithful friendship. It may be that Shakespeare created his character Cordelia with many classical and Christians values in mind. She's virtuous as she acts boldly upon her convictions, becoming a disruptive force of virtue in her father's headlong rush toward danger. She's full of mercy even after being brutally abused and rejected, and she pours out a reckless measure of forgiveness on her suffering father, which results in his dramatic and unexpected healing.


## The Simplest Acts

The vocation of friendship is a high calling that involves many challenges and many blessings. It's important to remember that the men and women we serve as friends have the same needs that we have. As Bonhoeffer writes, our friends need help, encouragement, and forgiveness, and God has placed us in relationship to serve one another. Service to a friend often requires that we become disruptive, humbly yet boldly challenging errors or decisions that could result in trouble, harm, or even death. May God give us the courage and wisdom to be disruptive when necessary. Service to a friend may also require that we be agents of healing. We can offer healing to friends in many different ways. The healing we offer our friends may be in gracious and regular forgiveness, as it was for Cordelia. Bonhoeffer ranks listening and helpfulness as the top two ways one can offer healing service to a friend. He elevates the act of listening to divine levels when he writes, "It is God's love for us that he not only gives us is Word but also lends us his ear. So it is his work that we do for our brother when we learn to listen to him."[25]

Bonhoeffer describes the helpfulness of a friend as something that must never be forced and that almost always begins with the simplest acts. It's not only important to always offer to help, but it's also important to wait to be invited to help. When a friend invites you to serve with her, she's entrusting you with something personal, no matter how trivial. As Bonhoeffer writes, "There is a multitude of these [trifling, external matters] wherever people live together. Nobody is too good for the meanest service. One who worries about the loss of time that such petty, outward acts of helpfulness entail is usually taking the importance of his own career too solemnly."[26] We can be awarded with praise for the helpfulness we offer the community around us. Many high school students join leadership organizations that require them to spend time doing community service.

When big, very public acts of service are required of us, we often find it exhilarating to give our best. However, the daily helpfulness we can offer friends may seem small and insignificant. It may be something that no one sees or recognizes. These are the acts of helpfulness that Bonhoeffer claims are the easiest to ignore, to pass by, and to brush off as a waste of time. It's often the simplest acts, however, that lead us to establish the deepest friendships.

Mother Teresa was famous for encouraging others to do small things, simple acts of service, with great love. In 2012, I had the opportunity to travel to India with Concordia University Irvine's Around-the-World Semester® program. Our team of students and professors spent two weeks in Kolkata working with Mother Teresa's Missionaries of Charity. The home I worked in was dedicated to the rehabilitation and care of men who suffered with severe disabilities. Many of the men couldn't walk, and they needed help with basic functions. On my first day of service, I was asked to help a man named Salam get to the bathroom and to take a shower. This was awkward for me at first, and although I thought I would be better suited for other kinds of work, I stuck with it. After the first few days of carrying Salam to the bathroom, I realized that I had been invited into something sacred and profound. Salam had offered me friendship by inviting me into his suffering and need. While I helped Salam get back and forth to the bathroom and to the shower, we shared stories about our families, our childhood, and even some of our dreams for the future. It was through a very simple act of helpfulness that Salam and I became friends. At the end of my time in Kolkata, I was overwhelmed with gratitude, and I thanked God for helping me see beyond my own self-importance.

The vocation of friendship is a divine calling that we must embrace with courage and humility. The Spice Girls sang some important truths about this significant and powerful relationship. The ancient philosophers Aristotle and Cicero provided us with some important ideas to consider about friendship and virtue, and Shakespeare's Cordelia gave us a snapshot of friendship in action. In the teachings of Jesus, we found divine friendship as well as some strong encouragement to extend grace and friendship to others. Christian friendship departs from the mutual benefits, the give-and-take, usually associated with secular views of friendship, and it makes possible the elevation and restoration of inequalities through personal sacrifice, forgiveness, and grace. While Aristotle and Cicero emphasize the importance of treating friends as second selves, friendship with Christ offers something transcendent. In Christ, we find a friend who has given his life for us, and in his sacrifice, we receive true spiritual healing and eternal life.

No matter where you are in your journey of faith, it's valuable to recognize the important ways that friendships push us beyond self-serving comfort and pleasure and toward a mutual exchange of disruptions and benefits that God is using to heal us and help us know him. God created the vocation of friendship, fully expressed by Christ, as a means by which we know God and as a way to serve one another.

## Exercises for Reflection and Discussion

1. Name two or three popular songs or films that focus on the topic of friendship. What do the artists believe is most important about friendship? Do you agree?
2. Describe a time when you were disrupted by someone like Cordelia or received healing in a friendship. How did that act of friendship help you? Create a card, video, or handwritten letter to give to your friend, thanking them for that gift of friendship.
3. Which of your current friends can you help today? What does he or she need most from you? Is it a listening ear, a spoken truth, or an act of kindness, such as encouragement or forgiveness?
4. Who have you met recently that needs you to be his or her friend? What simple acts could you do to befriend him or her?

## Notes

1 Gene Edward Veith, *God at Work: Your Christian Vocation in All of Life* (Wheaton, IL: Crossway, 2002), 19.
2 Veith, 33.
3 C. S. Lewis, *The Four Loves* (1960; repr., San Francisco: HarperOne, 2017), 73.

4  Lewis, 75.

5  Martin Luther, "Sermons on the Gospel of St. John, Chapter 15," in *Luther's Works*, American Edition, 55 vols., ed. Jaroslav Pelikan and Helmut T. Lehmann (Philadelphia: Muehlenberg and Fortress / St. Louis: Concordia, 1955–86), 24:253.

6  Matthew Harrison, *Christ Have Mercy: How to Put Your Faith in Action* (St. Louis: Concordia, 2008), 254.

7  Harrison, 255.

8  Spice Girls, "Wannabe," by Spice Girls, Matt Rowe, and Richard Stannard; performed by Spice Girls, recorded December 1995, track 1 on *Spice*, Virgin Records, compact disc.

9  Aristotle, *The Nicomachean Ethics*, trans. Lesley Brown (Oxford: Oxford University Press, 2009), 178.

10  Cicero, *De Amicitia (On Friendship)*, trans. Andrew P. Peabody (Boston: Little, Brown, 1887), 23. This edition can be accessed online at http://lf-oll.s3.amazonaws.com/titles/544/0267_Bk.pdf.

11  Cicero, 18.

12  Luther, "Sermons on the Gospel," 251.

13  Luther, "Sermons on the Gospel," 252.

14  Dietrich Bonhoeffer, *Life Together*, trans. John W. Doberstein (San Francisco: HarperOne, 2009), 24–25.

15  Citations for *King Lear* note the act, scene, and line(s) being quoted. The edition of *King Lear* used here is from David Bevington's *The Complete Work of Shakespeare*, 4th ed. (New York: HarperCollins, 1992).

16  David Konstan, *Friendship in the Classical World* (Cambridge: Cambridge University Press, 1997), 3.

17  Aristotle, *Nicomachean Ethics*, 177.

18  Cicero, *De Amicitia*, 17.

19  Cicero, 62.

20  Cicero, 62.

21  Bonhoeffer, *Life Together*, 105.

22  Bonhoeffer, 106.

23  Cicero, *De Amicitia*, 18–19.

24  Bonhoeffer, *Life Together*, 111–12.

25  Bonhoeffer, 97.

26  Bonhoeffer, 99.

# Take a Load off and Take a Look Around

*Ken Sundet Jones*

## "Well-Spring of the Joy of Living"

Henry van Dyke wrote the text of the hymn "Joyful, Joyful We Adore Thee" in 1907 while staying at the home of a college president. It's full of sunny praise to God for all the places we see God in the world around us. Its final verse could serve as a brief coda to what you've been reading about vocation in this book:

> Thou art giving and forgiving, ever blessing, ever blest,
> Well-spring of the joy of living, ocean depth of happy rest!
> Thou our Father, Christ our brother, all who live in love are thine;
> Teach us how to love each other, lift us to the joy divine.[1]

We could leave it at that: in our various vocations, a gracious God calls us to serve our neighbors, and in the midst of this service, we gain a glimpse of Christ's own service to us.

But there's one more piece we need to speak of. It's connected to the second line of the verse: "Well-spring of the joy of living, ocean depth of happy rest!" Our existence and purpose in this world are intimately connected to our relationships with others, yet God is also working in our lives to provide both joy and rest. In some cultures, Epiphany, the festival remembering the visit of the Magi to the baby Jesus (see Matthew 2:1–12), is celebrated by baking a loaf of *rosca de reyes* (three-kings bread). The loaf is filled with candied fruit, drizzled with icing, and formed to the shape of a crown. Hidden inside is a tiny porcelain figure of the infant Christ. If vocation is a loaf of tasty three-kings bread, then joy and rest are the surprises hidden within that make living a true delight.

## Free for Gladness

In his 1520 treatise on Christian freedom, the reformer Martin Luther described life with two contradictory statements: "The Christian individual is a completely free lord of all, subject to none. The Christian individual is a completely dutiful servant of all, subject to all."[2] Up to this point in this book, most of what you've read has to do with the second statement about being in service to your neighbor.

But what about all that freedom Luther said life also consists of? Freedom is one of the most important gifts young people can encounter—including those who have no particular faith commitment. For Luther, to be free is to no longer be bound by demands of the moral gatekeepers masquerading in religious language. Being free means gaining access to a realm of delight that you can explore. Theologian Mark Mattes says it creates an appreciation for the world and its beauty: when we're liberated from needing to earn God's favor, we can "enjoy an aesthetic of freedom, loving God for his own sake, others for their own sakes, and appreciating creation as a gift."[3]

The creation we're surrounded by is endlessly delightful, and being a creature in it provides equally endless joy and gladness. A world that contains such variety and symmetry is a world that can be watched with amusement and studied with scientific interest. In the book of Genesis, the name of the garden in which our first parents are placed is Eden, which can be translated as "delight." We live in the midst of a garden of earthly delights: the intricate combination of pitches that blend into a Mozart piano sonata; the way tendons and ligaments, muscles and bones are knit together to form a limb; how words join to form the wildly different poems of Robert Service and Mary Oliver; and the perfect blend of tastes and textures that wind up as a dish of Cajun red beans and rice. God's intention is not only that we live within the delight of his gracious attention but also that we delight in the world in which we live, including our own bodies (ear lobes, appendix, and uvula) and communities (all those vocations we've looked at so far).

What you take delight in does matter in the realm of vocation. The classic Frederick Buechner definition of vocation talks about your joy. He says your vocation is the place "where your deep gladness and the world's deep hunger meet."[4] When it comes to vocation, the problem with the definition is that deep gladness *might* arise from service to others, but it can just as easily feel like you're connecting to your passion, especially when you know the Latin word *passio* means "suffering." Living your vocation may give you gladness, but serving others can also feel like suffering. That's because service requires that we give up something of ourselves, whether it's our money, status, or life itself.

In his story "Crazy Mary Katherine,"[5] Martin Bell tells of a faithful woman who temporarily resided in a mental institution. Some thoughtful church ladies show up, doing their best to fulfill Jesus' words about visiting the sick (see Matthew 25:36). After some small talk, the visitors inform Mary Katherine about the upcoming church fund-raising campaign, and they tell her they hope she'll contribute because it'll make her feel good. They assume that "God loves a cheerful giver" (2 Corinthians 9:7). Mary Katherine replies that she'll certainly give but refuses to be cheerful about it. In her mind, there's no doubt that "giving is dying," and she can't imagine a sane person finding anything cheerful about doing it. In spite of Mary Katherine's logic, Jesus said, "Greater love has no one than this, that someone lay down his life for his friends" (John 15:13). But if your life includes being free to experience the gladness of being a creature, then your gladness can also lead to all kinds of interesting projects, quirky paths, and surprising connections to the world around you.

## The Making of an Enthusiast

When my son Sam was four years old, we took him to the local fair in Winneshiek County, Iowa. From that day onward, he was taken up by the deep gladness of roller coasters. He became obsessed with air-time, speed, and g-forces. He stowed away facts in his young brain about wood and steel, suspended and looping, standing and drop coasters. He knew the height, manufacturer, and date of construction for just about any machine in the US. We paid for a family membership to the American Coaster Enthusiasts and journeyed cross-country to be part of their annual CoasterCon.

I found myself standing in queues for coasters I knew would rattle me and inversions I knew I'd begin blacking out in. I registered for CoasterCounter.com to keep track of how many coasters I'd ridden (as of today, 231 coasters in 27 parks). I was drawn in because of my son's deep gladness, and because my own deepest place of gladness comes from being his dad. I've been able to observe how Sam became a walking database of all things coaster and amusement park. What's more, I saw how his delight has led to a life that goes beyond mere enjoyment.

In junior high school, Sam said he wanted to become a roller coaster designer. He had a spiral notebook in which he'd map out an imaginary and ideal amusement park, each page showing the layout of the park on successive years. You could see the shape and size both of the rides and of his imagination. The idea of being a coaster engineer came to an end when he learned that more people have walked on the moon than currently design coasters in the entire world. But the skills that were first honed in sketching his fantasy park's history morphed into something substantial. After college and a music degree, he became interested in urban planning and design. The same skills that his delight pulled him into now have a different purpose in his graduate program and his future work addressing housing and transportation questions in order to create walkable cities. Planning amusements morphed into planning sustainable places for people to live. The innocuous love of roller coasters honed something in him that allowed him to see the world in new ways.

## Three Avocations

The last word in "American Coaster Enthusiasts" is a good one for us to consider. The Greek roots of enthusiasm are the words *en* and *theos*, or "in" and "God." When we talk about salvation in terms of enthusiasm, it can lead us to think that our place in God's Kingdom depends on our feelings: accessing God within our emotions and experiences. That doesn't work well with the Christian claim that salvation comes from what Christ did for us. But the idea of enthusiasm can be a helpful consideration when it comes to our freedom in the world, especially if our delight opens us to see God present in what's around us.

At a recent church convention, I was bored by the proceedings and found myself visiting in the hallway with a retired pastor named Ed. We were talking about summer plans, and he said he had a driving trip to South Dakota on the docket. That's my home state, so I assumed he was heading to Mount Rushmore and the Black Hills or to a bit of fishing for northern pike on the Missouri River. But the pastor's reason for travel wasn't anything so naturally beautiful. He was going to the Great Plains because he and a friend collected counties.

It turns out there are lots of folks who count counties, and I was completely unaware of it. There's even a website where you can keep track of your count. I shouldn't have been surprised, given my own history with roller coasters. Ed had been to every county in the lower forty-eight states except for one in Hawaii, all of Alaska, and the twenty-two in Florida that he also had an itinerary for visiting in the summer.

That's a hobby that can lead to more than the county-tracking website shows. Ed has gotten to know the lay of the land—both geographically and socially—across a wide swath of this continent. He's interacted with the expansive variety of people who populate the space between the Atlantic and Pacific Oceans. And he's become more open to diversity, which changes how he interacts with people in his own daily sphere.

On any given Sunday morning, my friend Diane and I sit in pews on opposite sides of the aisle in our congregation. During the sermon, you'll find each of us with knitting needles in our hands, usually working on a pair of socks. Our hands keep moving in a way that pulls away other distractions so we can listen to the sermon. When I see the socks, sweaters, and shawls Diane has made, I'm amazed. I understand why the nearest knitting shop has her teaching classes. She not only creates beauty; she also pulls in other people and shows them how to do the same. And she does it with infinite patience, grace, and joy.

Taking up knitting has its own set of deeper outcomes. You begin to look for patterns in the things you wear—how the socks on your feet are constructed; how your Scandinavian mittens use two strands of yarn to make pictures of snowflakes; and how a T-shirt is actually the product of knitting with impossibly thin yarn and tiny needles. In order to create a knitted stuffed animal or cardigan vest, you have to be willing to make mistakes and seek help to correct the flaws. Diane has always saved the day when I've come to her with a dropped stitch or to express my frustration at tearing out the last ten rows of knitting. Her deep gladness has crafted a diligence that sees something to completion and translates to diligence in enduring things like friendships and family.

When I was in college, I auditioned for and made it into my college's highly regarded choir. In the Lutheran choral world, that's a big accomplishment. But at the second rehearsal I attended, I was deleted from the choir roster in favor of a senior who'd sung in the tenor section the previous year and wanted back in. I mistakenly took that as a negative assessment of my singing abilities, and it took me another thirty years to find my way back into a choir. This last year, a friend finally cajoled me enough and spoke such praises of its director that I relented and joined the Drake University Community Chorus. Each Tuesday evening of the school year, 120-plus community members meet for rehearsals under Eric Barnum to prepare for two concerts during the school year. This is a diverse set of people: vibrant university students earning course credit, grounded young professionals making time in hectic schedules, retirees whose voices aren't as strong as they once were and who might need to sit in a chair rather than stand on risers, and a timid singer like me. But they all commit their time and focus their energies on filling the hall with sound.

In weekly rehearsal and our final concert, I discovered that we were creating what the music conductor Weston Noble called a "special world."[6] Choral singing is unlike any other singing, whether it's leading a praise band at church, banging your head to "Bohemian Rhapsody" while tooling down the freeway, or nakedly warbling an aria in your shower. In a choir, you can't think only about the line your section is singing. You have to consider how your part is contributing to the whole sound at any given moment in the piece you're working on. You're producing something that individuals can't make on their own. Because I'm so engaged in thinking about the sound, whatever has burdened me during the day is sloughed off in rehearsal. The individual me becomes an integral part of the whole, and my cares and worries diminish in the face of Noble's special world. The listening and harmonizing, the notes, the chords, the rests, and the individual voices all come together to make sound convey emotion and truth. They confect a moment, an experience that transcends the mundane.

## Enthusiasm *Not* Hedonism

On the surface, each of these avocations is self-focused. We take up hobbies, crafts, sports, and enthusiasms because they please us. But mere pleasure isn't reason enough to engage in them. In a culture that regards our gladness and pleasure as ends in themselves, we need to gobble up our delight with a grain of salt.

Our culture preaches a daily sermon of pleasure for its own sake. It regards the purpose of life as collecting more life, more experiences, more happiness, and more pleasure and ease. But that's hedonism, a self-indulgence that regards your own happiness as paramount. And it's made worse in a tempting digital world of smart devices, incessant screens, news tickers, texting, and social media. It all seeks to grab your attention and squeezes out dopamine into your brain to bring you that instant shot of pleasure. It all puts the focus on you.

But your gladness and joy can have other ends. As you engage in your avocations and enthusiasms, you can begin to spot the intricate weave of the Creator's hand at play in your encounters with the creation. The story of the man and woman in Eden says that "out of the ground the LORD God made to spring up every tree that is pleasant to the sight and good for food" (Genesis 2:9). Hidden behind the visible things you can spot with your eyes are God's pleasure and goodness lying in wait for your attention. In the Old Testament, the psalmist looks up at the ancient nighttime skies without light pollution and sees the array of stars in the Milky Way as evidence of God's hand at work: "When I look at your heavens, the work of your fingers, the moon and the stars, which you have set in place, what is man that you are mindful of him, and the son of man that you care for him?" (Psalm 8:3–4). The whole of the cosmos is a place you can be enthusiastic about because God is there in it. Delight and deep gladness in what you spot in the world and the God you find behind this mask can take you outside yourself. You're stretched out so that you're no longer curved in on yourself, staring eternally and sinfully at your own navel.

The skills that come with your joyous participation in the world can lead to something greater. No matter what place your deep gladness occurs, your avocations and enthusiasms can be the seeds from which service of an abiding and satisfying sort can sprout. When that happens, then your neighbor and the world itself reap an abundant harvest from what you initially might have thought of as simply messing around or a waste of time. It's like the tiny mustard seed in Jesus' parable that's planted and grows up into a towering home for birds to make nests in its branches (see Matthew 13:31–32).

## Ocean Depth of Happy Rest

In the story of the Exodus, God calls the Israelite Moses to lead God's enslaved people out of bondage in Egypt into the freedom of the Promised Land. After all the back-and-forth with Pharaoh, ten increasingly dire plagues, a by-the-skin-of-our-teeth escape from Egypt's charioteers at the Red Sea, and forty years wandering in the wilderness, at last, Moses watched his people journey into Canaan. Along the way, Moses began to think he was indispensable. At the Red Sea, the waters parted when he lifted up *his* hands. Striking the rock with *his* staff brought water for the parched Israelites. From dawn to dusk he was the one who had to judge all the disputes among the people. Finally, his father-in-law, Jethro, came to Moses with a probing question, like the one that Chad Lakies points to in the "Identity: A Task or Given?": "What is this that you are doing for the people? Why do you sit alone, and all the people stand around you from morning till evening?" Jethro told Moses the truth: "What you are doing is not good. You and the people with you will certainly wear yourselves out, for the thing is too heavy for you" (Exodus 18:14, 17–18).

What Jethro understood is also the reason behind the third commandment, "Remember the Sabbath day, to keep it holy" (Exodus 20:8). If you work and work and work without ever taking time off, you'll wind up in a boring rut at best. At worst, you'll plow a path that leads to your grave. When it comes to vocation, burnout is a distinct possibility. Your neighbors' needs are endless, and their voices crying out are so plaintive and strong. Burnout happens when you don't take a break.

When the commandments show up later in the Israelites' history, the Sabbath commandment is focused primarily on worship in the Temple (see, for instance, Leviticus 19:1–7). But the earliest places the commandments appear seem to be aimed at precisely this need for rest. The Sabbath commandment prohibits all agricultural work. You weren't even allowed a fire to prepare meals. When the prophet Amos was preaching, the merchants in cities complained that this commandment had been applied to them (see Amos 8:4–6). Amos responded by bringing the Lord's hammer down with a prophecy of gloom and doom for those who broke the commandment.[7] It wasn't that long ago that most cities and states in our country had "blue laws." These laws said that on Sundays, stores couldn't be open, liquor couldn't be sold, and car buyers had to shop the other six days of the week.

Although we've mostly abandoned the idea of the Sabbath in our day, there's wisdom in those ancient practices. We live in a world that demands that you justify yourself through productivity. In past eras, we might have tried to justify ourselves via religious practices, but the subtitle of David Zahl's recent book points to the things that are the fire at both ends of our candles, depleting us daily: *Seculosity: How Career, Parenting, Technology, Food, Politics, and Romance Became Our New Religion and What to Do about It*.[8] Zahl argues that in our day, we've turned to these things, which are certain components of a life of vocation, into ends in themselves. The culture around us puts a premium on being busy, and it becomes a badge of honor to be able to bemoan how you're being crucified by the calendar app on your phone.

The pressure on college students to perform is immense. The almighty GPA is the golden calf that everyone bows down to. Heaven forfend if a paper yields an average grade! It leads students to worry about winding up outside the professional world and the fear of a life of drudgery working as a cashier in a red shirt and tan pants at the local big-box retailer. The win-loss bottom line is at the forefront of student-athletes' minds. My university now has nine straight championships. The dual wins and string of pins and major decisions are great, but the pressure to perform on the mat is breathtaking. Do we even need to mention the demands for performance in a campus hookup culture? On my campus, there's a reason we talk about the last week of the semester as "dead week." As a professor, it's easy for me to read a sloppy essay and think, Would it kill ya to actually proofread something before you turn it in? But I know that for some students, that one extra step before submitting a paper simply isn't possible, because they're at the end of their academic ropes.

## Take a Load Off

Moses's father-in-law wanted him to open his eyes and see what he was doing to himself. The lie of constant work as a source of life had to be uncloaked, and the truth had to be told. When God gives the commandments to Moses atop Mount Sinai, the third commandment about the Sabbath day reminds us that we have a God who's capable of eternal toil but *still* takes a break: "For in six days the LORD made heaven and earth, the sea, and all that is in them, and rested on the seventh day. Therefore the LORD blessed the Sabbath day and made it holy" (Exodus 20:11). The commandment is given so that we aren't killed by our work. God would probably give a divine thumbs-up to Robbie Robertson's "The Weight," the classic song by The Band from 1968: "Take a load off Annie / Take a load for free / Take a load off Annie / And you put the load right on me."[9]

This rest is countercultural. To have an avocation, something you're enthusiastic about, is to thumb your nose at the performance metrics the world uses to judge your value. Especially when you know that God has promised to provide everything needed for life. Such a sense of enoughness gives the freedom Luther was after. It frees you to stop taking the world's demands and your own self so seriously. The reformer regarded those demands as the Devil's work. In a letter to a law enforcement officer suffering from melancholy, Luther recommended doing something useless and saying to your tempter, "Well, devil, do not trouble me. I have no time for your thoughts. I must eat, drink, ride, go, or do this or that. . . . Come back tomorrow." If the pressure continued, Luther said, it might do to speak coarsely: "Dear Devil, if you can't do better than that, then kiss my ass, etc. I can't wait on you."[10]

If the "tiny skull-sized kingdom"[11] you live in places all the emphasis on attaining wealth and license to do whatever your heart desires and if the pressure to grab those golden rings bears down on you, it may be time to take up some useless activity. It might be heading to the gym for a pickup game of basketball. It might mean going old school and downloading a Tetris app to twiddle your thumbs at. Maybe it's the glory of being pampered in a mani-pedi joint. Perhaps it's being a Nerdfighter pushing back at the dominant cult of popularity and performance by reveling in whatever quirky thing fascinates you.[12]

My friend Willie is a pastor in a small, rural town in Iowa. He's one of the emotionally healthiest pastors I know, and he gets the benefits of rest better than anyone else I know. He bears all the burdens we place on any member of the clergy. He studies Scripture and prepares weekly sermons. He counsels the troubled. He visits the ill. He marries, baptizes, and buries his people. He serves in an important vocation, but the calling can become a burden for even the most faithful of pastors. I love watching how Willie lives his life within his community and family, for he's a man of many avocations and great enthusiasms.

Willie really would have fit in better in an earlier era, and if our society fell apart, I suspect he'd be someone who would thrive in a world disconnected from digital dominance. His Sabbath comes not only in his Sunday afternoon nap but also in bits and pieces across his days. He plays a mean alto sax. He recently posted a list of the twenty different varieties of chili peppers he planted this year, all of which will join the fourteen varieties of tomatoes he's also planted and become jar after jar of explosive salsa at the end of the growing season. They'll be on the shelves next to the sauerkraut he's fermented. In his freezer are jerky, pastrami, roasts, and deer sticks that are the result of his hunting. And any Sunday you attend worship at his church, you'll have bread in the Lord's Supper that Willie has

mixed, kneaded, and baked. It's the extracurriculars and his sense
of enoughness that keep my friend balanced. The balance gives him
a greater ability to take on his vocations as a husband, dad, pastor,
thinker, citizen, and resident of the world.

Learning your way around a ball of dough, a bread pan, and
an oven could be a path to your own balance. Mixing and kneading
those cheeks of dough, watching the yeast slowly proof and increase
the dough, baking it, and then slicing and slathering it with butter
and honey—these things take you out of yourself. Like the members
of the Drake choir earlier who lose themselves in their music, bak-
ers of bread have to get out of their own heads and simply trust that
their activity is pleasing and useful. Thumping the top of some risen
dough to test its elasticity forces you for the briefest of moments to
focus not on how your bread might please someone else's palate.
Instead, the dough asks to be the center of attention, the thing most
needful at that moment. And you lose your place in the equation.
Jesus said, "Whoever loses his life for my sake and the gospel's will
save it" (Mark 8:35). Surely that points us to serving others in our
vocations, but could it also have another meaning? Couldn't losing
yourself also be about being freed from the world's demands?

## A Sigh of Relief

For Christians, being connected to the gospel is central to their
identity. In his letter to the Galatians, Paul declared, "For freedom
Christ has set us free; stand firm therefore, and do not submit again
to a yoke of slavery" (Galatians 5:1). Christians regard an encounter
with the person of Christ as an event that bestows freedom from
the world's bondage. Experiencing that freedom is the kind of thing
that makes you go, "Aaaahhh. At last." It's an even deeper rest than
just taking a day off or having a hobby can give you. It's a kind of
rest that is a release from the forces Luther pointed to: sin, death,
and the Devil.

This is why worship is part of our vocations. We could call
worship an enthusiasm because God chooses to be found wherever
divine mercy is proclaimed in the name of Jesus. You might speculate
about God's presence on the golf course or the dance floor, in a red-
wood forest, or on a Carolina beach, but you'll also have to take God

in flooding, tornadoes, and earthquakes. But if you want to know for sure what God is up to, it means getting yourself to the place that exists to give you Christ's gifts. When you encounter Jesus' welcome and forgiveness of sinners in preaching and the sacraments, God places himself in you.[13] You're *en theos*—an enthusiast, in the best meaning of the word. This is why Luther says we become "a kind of Christ" to each other.[14] And now avocation, enthusiasm, and rest have taken us back to the central idea: we exist to serve one another, to be beacons of light and bearers of mercy. The reason for living is to give up our lives and receive them back in return.

The world regards the gospel of mercy in Christ—the "one little Word (that subdues evil)" in the Reformation hymn "A Mighty Fortress Is Our God"—as impotent and useless.[15] It would rather puff itself up with individual accomplishments and successes and see the small things inherent in relationships, in beauty, and in truth as inconsequential. Christianity has a horrible business plan. Being called to give up yourself isn't a good marketing ploy. Our world of commerce is little different from the markets where the merchants vented their spleen to the prophet Amos. Where the goal of success and a life of striving to produce enough hold sway, you won't find what Jesus called "ears to hear" (Mark 4:9). It's the places of need and the times when you let loose of your power and status for the sake of others in your web of relationships that real, honest-to-goodness life happens.

When you take a breather—whether through a mini-Sabbath of avocation that creates some joy in you or in the deeper rest of forgiveness declared in worship—you can't stay there forever. You'll always be drawn back to the world and your neighbors' needs. But your enthusiasms can be places where God takes the mask of vocations off to renew you, enlighten you, and equip you. Kids playing with Barbie dolls, your grandmother planting Petunias, the boots and backpacks that trace the Pacific Crest Trail, the college student learning to swim, the middle-aged guy with a dad bod shooting free throws, and a night out at a comedy club—these aren't useless pursuits. These are places where God surreptitiously moves to give you gladness, connection to the creation, and grounding. Go beneath the surface of your joy and gladness to see the changes God brings you through to create someone even more fit to serve. Take a load off.

Breathe. And then look around for whoever is next in line for the
gifts you bring to the world.

## Exercises for Reflection and Discussion

1. What are your avocations and enthusiasms? What skills lie
   behind those activities that might be honed and used elsewhere in your various vocations?
2. Zahl's book *Seculosity* points to six components of life that
   make relentless demands on us: careers, parenting, technology, food, politics, and romance. Put each component on a
   separate sticky note or index card and post them on a wall.
   Where do you see these things wearing you down and taking
   away life rather than giving it? Write your observations on the
   notes or cards. Over the next week, add new observations as
   they come to mind.
3. How can forgiveness—whether from another person or from
   God—secure your future in that relationship? How does it
   free you to explore your web of relationships with deep gladness? Share your ideas with a partner. If you have an example
   from your life to illustrate this, share that too.

## Notes

1 Henry van Dyke, "Joyful, Joyful We Adore Thee" (1907), in *Lutheran
  Book of Worship* (Minneapolis: Augsburg Fortress, 2006), 551.
2 Martin Luther, "The Freedom of a Christian" (1520), in *The Annotated
  Luther*, vol. 1, *The Roots of Reform*, trans. Timothy J. Wengert
  (Minneapolis: Fortress, 2016), 488.
3 Mark C. Mattes, *Martin Luther's Theology of Beauty: A Reappraisal*
  (Grand Rapids: Baker Academic, 2017), 162–63.
4 Frederick Buechner, *Wishful Thinking: A Theological ABC* (1973; repr.,
  New York: Harper & Row, 1993), 85.
5 Martin Bell, "Crazy Mary Katherine," in *Nenshu and the Tiger: Parables
  of Life and Death* (New York: Seabury, 1981).
6 Weston Noble, *Creating the Special World: A Collection of Lectures by
  Weston H. Noble* (Chicago: GIA, 2005).
7 See J. Morgenstern, "Sabbath," in *The Interpreter's Dictionary of the Bible*,
  vol. 4 (Nashville: Abingdon, 1962), 135 and following pages.

8 David Zahl, *Seculosity: How Career, Parenting, Technology, Food, Politics, and Romance Became Our New Religion and What to Do about It* (Minneapolis: Fortress, 2019).

9 The Band, "The Weight," by Robbie Robertson, performed by The Band, recorded early 1968, track 5 on *Music from Big Pink*, Capitol Records, compact disc.

10 Martin Luther, "Letter to Jonas von Stockhausen, November 27, 1532," in *D. Martin Luthers Werke: Kritische Gesamtausbage* (Weimar: Böhlau, 1883–1986), 6:388. My translation.

11 David Foster Wallace, "This Is Water," commencement address at Kenyon College, 2005.

12 The term comes from the young adult novelist John Green. On the website Nerdfighteria, it's defined this way: "Someone who, instead of being made out of bones and organs and stuff, is made entirely out of awesome. How do you know if you're a Nerdfighter? If you want to be one, then you are. (To clarify—a Nerdfighter does not fight nerds. A Nerdfighter fights *for* nerds.)" Accessed June 21, 2019, https://nerdfighteria.com/lexicon#N.

13 Sacraments are divinely instituted acts where God attaches his promises of mercy to physical elements that then convey God's grace and forgiveness in Christ to sinners. See, for instance, Jesus instituting the Lord's Supper (also known as Holy Communion or the Eucharist) in Matthew 26:26–29 and baptism in Matthew 28:19.

14 Luther, "Freedom of a Christian," 525.

15 Martin Luther, "A Mighty Fortress Is Our God" (late 1520s), in *Lutheran Book of Worship* (Minneapolis: Augsburg Fortress, 2006), 228.

Made in the USA
San Bernardino, CA
26 July 2020

76088732R00124